Amphissa from the south-east (Edward Lear, 1849).

Southern Greece:
An Archaeological Guide

Attica, Delphi and the Peloponnese

ROBERT AND KATHLEEN COOK

FABER AND FABER LIMITED
London : 24 Russell Square

First published in 1968
by Faber and Faber Limited
24 Russell Square, London, W.C.1
Printed in Great Britain
by Ebenezer Baylis and Son, Limited
The Trinity Press, Worcester, and London

SBN 571 08431 1

Contents

Illustrations

Mr H. A. Shelley has compiled Fig. 1 and copied or lettered and tidied most of the others.

Though based on standard publications, many of these plans are inaccurate in detail.

Acknowledgements

We have had much help in writing this book. For information, advice and correction we are indebted first to Professor E. Vanderpool, Mr A. W. Lawrence, Mr A. H. S. Megaw and Dr W. H. Plommer, then to Professor O. Broneer, Dr J. J. Coulton, Dr M. I. Finley, Mr P. Grierson, Mrs Eileen Hardie, Dr A. T. Hodge, Professor R. J. Hopper, Mr D. Limberis, Mr E. W. Marsden, Dr D. M. Nicol, Mr S. J. Papastavrou, Dr Judith Pinder, Miss Elizabeth Ramsden, Mr Stuart Rossiter, Mr G. B. Waywell, Dr C. K. Williams and many others. For providing illustrations and permission to publish them we mention (besides the names on the captions) Professor A. Greifenhagen, Dr Christiane Grunwald, Air Commodore A. F. Johnson, Mr D. Matthews, Dr Lucy Shoe Meritt, Professor Henry S. Robinson, Professor Homer A. Thompson and Dr F. R. Walton. Further, Mr H. A. Shelley, Mr S. C. Collard, Mr E. E. Jones and Mrs G. S. Blake have given much practical assistance. We thank them all most sincerely.

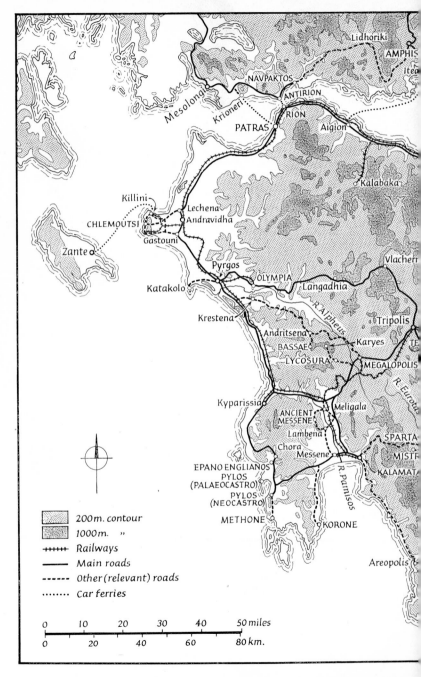

Fig. 1. Southern Greece.

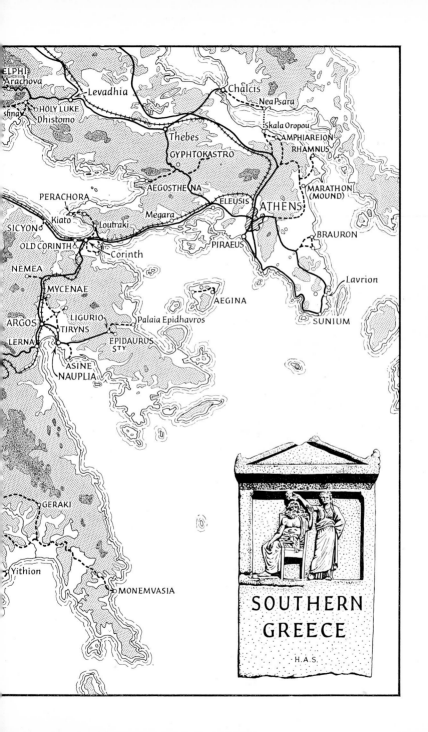

ELPHI
Arachova
Levadhia
Chalcis
Nea Psara
HOLY LUKE
Shnay
Dhistomo
Skala Oropou
Thebes
AMPHIAREION
GYPHTOKASTRO
RHAMNUS
PERACHORA
AEGOSTHENA
MARATHON
(MOUND)
ELEUSIS
ATHENS
Megara
SICYON
Kiato
Loutraki
Corinth
OLD CORINTH
PIRAEUS
BRAURON
NEMEA
Lavrion
MYCENAE
ARGOS
LIGURIO
AEGINA
TIRYNS
Palaia Epidhavros
LERNA
EPIDAURUS
SUNIUM
STY
ASINE
NAUPLIA

GERAKI

Yithion
MONEMVASIA

SOUTHERN
GREECE

H.A.S.

1 · Athens, the Acropolis

Most visitors to Greece stay too long in Athens. It has on the Acropolis the finest of Classical buildings and its museums contain the largest selection of antiquities, but the Renaissance did not come to Greece, the modern city is undistinguished and the setting must by Greek standards be reckoned mediocre. Those who prefer fresh air and quiet should stay outside, at Kifisia or on the coast, where too the sunsets are still worth seeing.

In any city which has been inhabited for millennia or enjoyed development in recent times ancient structures are lucky to survive and any systematic excavation of what remains below ground is difficult or impossible. So we are not likely to learn much more than we know now about early Athens. The original focus of settlement was the Acropolis, a steep-sided hill not too large or high and so convenient as a place of refuge, certainly till the cannon was invented. Mt Lycabettus, which to modern eyes looks a much more commanding position, was in ancient times always outside the city defences and is indeed mentioned very rarely in the surviving literature. So far the earliest traces of settlement are stray potsherds of the late Neolithic period, of say a little before 3000 B.C. It is not till the Late Bronze Age (the Mycenaean period) that we have any structural remains. Then the Acropolis was fortified with a wall and presumably contained a palace, there were houses below on the north side and wells and graves further down the slope. The later Greeks believed that the Dorian invaders (who are often supposed to have destroyed the Mycenaean regime) were beaten back from Attica, and certainly there is no interruption of the use of the Ceramicus cemetery or in the style of its burial goods. For the next four centuries, from the eleventh to the seventh, we have little except graves, wells and small objects, mostly pottery; nor does history—or rather the legends that pass for history—tell us anything more important. When around 600 B.C. the story becomes clearer, Athens was a growing city which had incorporated politically the whole of Attica. It is not known when this incorporation (or 'synoecism') happened. Legend gave the credit to

17

Theseus, who belonged to the Heroic (or Mycenaean) dream world, but some experts come down as late as the eighth century B.C. It is of course possible that the synoecism may have been gradual or not at first permanent. What is important is that it created one of the largest units of Archaic and Classical Greece, about as big as Cambridgeshire.

Although around 600 B.C. an area at the south of the Agora site was tidied up as a new civic centre and soon after stone temples and other public structures were built both there and on the Acropolis, Athens was suffering from economic and political troubles and about the middle of the sixth century, following the regular evolution of advanced Greek city states, it too had its tyrant or—in modern terminology—dictator. Whatever his motives Pisistratus gave settled government and encouraged production and, when the Spartans expelled his son and successor in 510 and aristocratic cliques were playing their old game, the citizens had acquired the capacity to take over control and Athens became a democracy (in the Greek sense of that word). Greek democracies were naturally aggressive, since the less solid citizens (who were in the majority) did not have enough property to benefit from peace and under-employment. Certainly the Athenian democracy profited by aggression. A rash intervention to help Greek rebels in Asia Minor provoked the Persian empire. The first attempt at reprisal was defeated at Marathon in 490. Ten years later the Persians returned in strength, this time overland and to conquer all Greece. Athens was evacuated but somehow enough of the Greek states combined to destroy the Persian fleet off Salamis and defeat their army at Plataea, and the invaders retreated. When in 479 the Athenians returned home, their city was in ruins but their reputation high and, as Sparta—the principal Greek power—proved reluctant, Athens with its new navy became the leader of a league of island and Asiatic Greeks in a war of liberation against Persia. Before long the Athenians turned the league into an empire and used part of the profits to beautify their city, especially the Acropolis. During the last third of the fifth century Athens was fighting Sparta for complete domination of the Greek world and, though it lost both the war and its empire, was still active and fairly prosperous well down the fourth century. Then the establishment of the Hellenistic kingdoms destroyed its political and much of its commercial importance, though not its cultural prestige. Whatever the faults of Athenian democracy, its patronage and intellectual climate had made Athens the metropolis of Greek art, literature and philosophy, assets as permanently valuable to itself as the outside world. Throughout the Hellenistic and

Roman epochs, however unwise its political decisions—one of which provoked Sulla's siege and partial sack of 86 B.C.—Athens remained the venerated shrine of Classical culture with its monuments, sculptors' workshops and philosophical schools and until the second century A.D. the rich intelligentsia of the ancient world competed in endowing it with new buildings and foundations or restoring old ones. When during the next century the Roman empire weakened and in A.D. 267 the Herulians sacked the lower city (but not the Acropolis), Athens made only a partial recovery; and when in 529 Justinian closed the schools of philosophy, the last refuge of paganism, the ancient city of culture was left to face the economic realities of the present. For the next thirteen hundred years Athens was never more than a modest market town. Till 1204 it remained an insignificant part of the Byzantine empire. Then it fell to the Franks, who set up what became the Duchy of Athens (with Thebes), and eventually passed to the Florentine family of the Acciajuoli. The Turks took Attica in 1456 and the Acropolis two years later, and except for a Venetian interlude from 1687–1688 remained masters of Athens till the War of Independence, finally departing in 1833. Next year the wretched town of some four thousand inhabitants became for the first time the capital of Greece. Now it is one of the big cities of Europe, with a population not far off two million.

The importance of Athens is one of the curiosities of history. Its natural advantages are not great, since it was neither on the sea nor on a main land route—Corinth and even Eleusis are better placed—nor is the country around rich in mineral wealth or particularly fertile. In the beginning the defensive merit of the Acropolis invited settlement and as the only good acropolis of the area Athens naturally became the stronghold of its plain. How Eleusis and the eastern part of Attica were annexed we cannot know, but once these areas were united Athens was conveniently central. The imperial prosperity of the fifth century B.C., even if supported by the silver mines of Laurium, came through the establishment of democracy and a naval policy, but both the causes and the result appear largely fortuitous. What is, though, clear is that the accompanying cultural achievement bolstered Athens till the third and even the sixth century A.D., and when in the nineteenth century Greece became independent it was again the cultural glories of the past, though then appreciated more in Western Europe than in Greece itself, which made Athens seem the predestined capital of the new state. Classical education has had strange consequences.

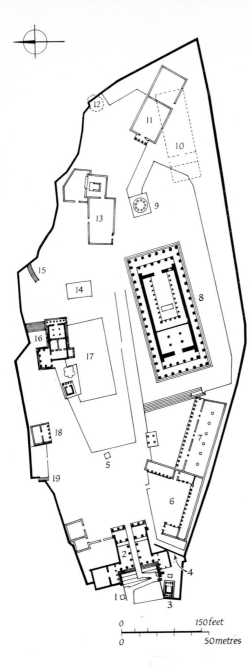

Fig. 2.

The Acropolis of Athens

Key to numbers:

1. MONUMENT OF AGRIPPA
2. PROPYLAEA
3. TEMPLE OF ATHENA NIKE
4. MYCENAEAN WALL
5. STATUE OF ATHENA PROMACHOS
6. BRAURONION
7. CHALKOTHEKE
8. PARTHENON
9. TEMPLE OF ROME
10. Museum
11. SANCTUARY OF PANDION
12. Belvedere
13. SANCTUARY OF ZEUS
14. ALTAR OF ATHENA
15. MYCENAEAN POSTERN
16. ERECHTHEUM
17. OLD NORTH TEMPLE
18. HOUSE OF ARREPHOROI
19. STAIRWAY

0 _____ 150 feet

0 _____ 50 metres

The Acropolis   (*Fig.* 2)

The Acropolis is the best place at which to begin the tour of Athens.
Till the middle of the fifth century B.C. it was and looked much more
rugged than it does now with the rock at the top levelled down and the
sides within the surrounding wall banked up. So, to take the most
notable example, part of the north side of the platform of the Parthenon
rests directly on the natural rock, which has also been dressed down, but
the south side is supported on a foundation more than 35 feet deep and,
as can be seen in the two modern pits, the slope continued downwards
to the base of the outer wall. For this knowledge of the unimproved
aspect of the hill we depend largely on the Greek excavations of 1885–90,
which stripped the accessible surface down to bed rock and incidentally
recovered from the fill most of the Archaic sculptures now in the
Acropolis Museum as well as a mass of pottery and bronze figurines.
Unfortunately the standards of the late nineteenth century were not
exacting and we cannot find out now what, if any, structural indications
may have been missed. Anyhow, the first known fortification of the
Acropolis was a stone wall built in the late Mycenaean period, probably
during the later thirteenth century. It followed the slope in an irregular
line, generally a little within the present wall. The best preserved stretch
that is visible now runs from the south side of the Propylaea past the
south-west wing to the edge of the rock. The main gate, which was
near-by, had the extra protection of a bastion on the spur which now
supports the Nike Temple; near the later sanctuary of the Arrephoroi
a staircase led down for a few years to a spring below and outside the
wall; and east of the Erechtheum there was a postern gate. The Mycenaean wall was kept in repair till the 460's, when a new and straighter
wall was built further out by Cimon and Pericles. This has been maintained ever since, till 1835 as a military fortification and afterwards as
an ancient monument. Generally the smaller and rougher the stones the
later is the date of construction.

The Propylaea

The main entrance to the Acropolis has always been from the west
though not always on the same alignment. The first monument as the
path goes up from the car-park is the Beulé Gate, so-called after the
French archaeologist who uncovered it. This is a defensive work of the
late third or fourth century A.D., but re-uses older material, particularly

Plate 1. Athens from the south-west (anonymous, 1670).

from the choregic monument which a Nicias dedicated in 320 B.C. (as its inscription records). Clumsily put together and obstructing the view of the Propylaea, it is a pity that this gate was not mistaken for Turkish and dismantled. Another unhappy excrescence is the Monument of Agrippa, a towering pedestal higher up on the left. This was erected about 174 B.C. to support a bronze chariot, but had at least two diplomatic changes of use; at one time it carried statues of Antony and Cleopatra, then when Augustus eliminated them his friend Agrippa was awarded their place.

The Propylaea is a double six-columned porch with side wings, all of white marble now oxidised to brown. It was designed by Mnesicles and built between 437 and 432 B.C., though like many Greek buildings never completed; perhaps, as is usual, the architect underestimated or funds did not come in. Heliodorus, writing in the second century B.C., made the bill for the Propylaea 2012 talents or rather more than 12,000,000 days' wages for a skilled craftsman, but reasonable costing suggests that the figure may be as much as ten times too high. In the Middle Ages the building was converted to new uses. It became the residence of the Orthodox Archbishop, the chancery and later the palace of the Frankish and Florentine Dukes, who also built a high tower on the south (*Plate* 1) —one may meditate on Bottom producing his tragical comedy of

'Pyramus and Thisbe' in this setting—and the Turks used it both for the governor's residence and as a powder magazine, which was struck by lightning and exploded about 1650. In the nineteenth century the Greeks cleared away the various alterations and accretions, and more recently have done some helpful restoration.

If funds allowed, the entrance to a Greek sanctuary was normally dignified by a pair of gabled porches, one on each side of the gate. Here not only was something specially grand desired, but there was also the difficulty of an unusually steep slope. At ground level it was easy enough to manage this by steps but the axes of the roof had to be horizontal and the Greeks did not like a stepped roof. Mnesicles' solution was to raise the outer porch on a highish foundation and make the columns of the eastern face a little shorter than those of the western. This left the roof at the east still nearly 5 feet higher than that at the west but, since the west porch was very deep, the awkward junction came so far back that it was not noticeable from any viewpoint on the ground. A similar attention to visible effect rather than to theoretical elevation and planning is evident in the two wings, originally hip-roofed, which stand high above the outer approach. Each offers the spectator a facade with three Doric columns, set between antae (or piers); but though the facades are symmetrical, the structures behind them are not. The north-west wing or Pinakotheke (that is the gallery or store for pictures) is a deep rectangular building with vestibule and back room, but the south-west wing is shallow and open to the west and the terminal pier of its colonnade was connected only by the entablature and a narrow strip of roof. This ingenious sham to balance the facades of the two wings shocks some critics and it is often asserted that the original project was for a south-west wing exactly corresponding to the Pinakotheke, but the opposition of the priests of Artemis Brauronia (on whose ground this wing might have encroached) forced its subsequent curtailment. It is true that on the east side of the Propylaea two flanking structures were intended, as can be seen from the preparation of the adjoining wall-ends, though we do not know whether they were to be of equal size, but the hypothesis about the western wings is neither necessary nor particularly probable. The nearest position from which their asymmetry can be seen at all clearly is more than 300 yards away on the hill opposite and from there the Nike bastion blocks the view of the south-west wing, while the face of the Pinakotheke looks like an independent building rather than a part of the gateway.

The ingenuity and the quality of design and workmanship in the

Propylaea are remarkable. Classical architecture followed a fairly rigid system of proportions, which had developed in such simple buildings as temples and was not convenient for more complex structures. Very properly the colonnades of the western wings are smaller in scale than that of the dominant entrance porch, but the size of steps was related to the size of the columns above them and yet appearances demanded that the flights of the porch and the wings should be continuous. Mnesicles compromised with a continuous flight of four steps of which the lowest on the sides was of dark stone, so that the eye would find a satisfactory ratio between the total height of the four steps and the columns of the porch and between the three white steps and the columns of the wings. At least this is the most reasonable explanation of the use of dark stone, an uncommon practice in Greek building. Dark stone is used also for the top step at the gates themselves, perhaps as a warning to anyone coming in from the bright sunlight outside or to emphasise the threshold of the sacred precinct of the Acropolis. Another oddity is the eccentric placing of the door and two windows in the Pinakotheke, for which the only suggestions worth considering are that they were intended to be seen from a particular turn on the path up or to prevent direct sunlight falling on the pictures. In the main building the span of the side passage-ways, just over 16 feet, was dangerously wide by Greek standards; so the central architraves were hollowed out and iron bars inserted to transfer to the columns the load of the intermediate ceiling beams. The combination of Doric columns outside and Ionic inside the western porch is normal in Classical buildings (such as stoas) where a ceiling needs support; ceiling beams are one or two courses higher than architraves and the slimmer proportions of Ionic columns allow a greater height for the same or, as here, a lesser diameter. Both these sets of columns are excellent in themselves, and the Ionic capitals are unsurpassed. The coffered ceiling, which was particularly admired by Pausanias, still shows traces of painted decoration, a characteristic of ancient architecture that is too easily ignored. All these parts are exquisitely finished, but on much of the walls the surface has not been trimmed down except at the edges and outside at the east many of the wall blocks still keep the bosses by which they were hauled into position. Such blemishes, common enough in the best Greek architecture, do not include the ugly sockets for ceiling beams which disfigure the south side of the central hall; classical sockets as can be seen in several parts of the propylaea are neatly squared, but these were hacked out by the Floren-tines or Franks.

The original approach to the Propylaea was by a zigzag path, of which the modern causeway though too low gives some idea. The imposing stairway, which this cuts, was installed in the mid first century A.D., as if to demonstrate the Roman disposition towards grandiose axial compositions and the Greek preference for a deliberate casualness in the grouping of buildings. The prospect from the other side must have been considered too, even though the Parthenon was there already and so the favourite oblique view for a temple was pre-determined. For the most convenient natural approach was presumably that of the older Propylaea, which faced the site later occupied by the Erechtheum; instead Mnesicles chose an axis nearer but still not on the median line of the Acropolis and with no important structure encroaching on it. The Propylaea is an exceptionally fine and instructive example of Classical architecture, so that it is worth spending some time there; it also makes a convenient halfway stage in the ascent of the Acropolis.

Temple of Athena Nike

The charming little marble Temple of Nike (or, to give it its full title, Athena Nike) is reached from the Propylaea through the south-west wing, which makes an effective portico in front of it. The site had its altar and cult long before the present building was put up, probably about 425 B.C. and just after the Propylaea, with which of course it is not in alignment. The temple was lucky. Somehow it survived the Middle Ages and just before the Venetian siege of 1687, when artillery was becoming more destructive, the Turks took it down and used its blocks to build a battery. Reconstruction was done very competently in the 1830's. The Nike Temple is in the specialist terminology tetrastyle amphiprostyle, that is it has a porch of four columns at each end: a continuous colonnade or 'peristyle' was usual only with largish temples of some elaboration. The style is Ionic of the superior species not found so early in Ionia; characteristic are the bases of the columns and the sculptured frieze. In front of the temple there was a sizable altar, and the sides and back of the platform were protected by a parapet with figures of Nike (Victory) carved on the outer face. The remains of this Nike Balustrade are in the Museum.

The Parthenon

The Parthenon dominates the Acropolis from most viewpoints. It was begun under the direction of the architects Ictinus and Callicrates in

447 B.C. and finished in nine years. In the sixth century A.D. it was converted into a church and, since Pagan temples and Christian churches faced opposite ways, a door was cut through the back wall of the cella and an apse inserted at the east; either then or on some earlier occasion the interior colonnades were replaced. The Franks changed the rite from Greek to Roman. The Turks about 1460 made the few changes necessary for a mosque and added a minaret at the south-west (*Plate* 1). Though these adaptations did some damage to the interior, they should not be regretted too much, since except in remote and deserted regions an ancient building did not have much chance of surviving, unless it continued to be useful. What was disastrous was the Venetian siege of 1687, when the attackers learnt that gunpowder was being stored in the Parthenon and a well-placed cannon-ball blew up the interior and parts of both sides of the outer colonnade. Afterwards the Turks built a small mosque inside the ruins and did some casual damage. Clearance and restoration began when the Greeks took over in the 1830's and still continue to the horror of purists, though the recent rebuilding of the sides of the outer colonnade, by uniting the two disconnected ends, is an advantage to the visitor who sees with his eyes rather than his imagination.

The present Parthenon was not the first temple on the site. In the sixth century B.C. and presumably earlier there were two principal temples on the Acropolis, one here and the other just south of the Erechtheum. They are now called indiscriminately the Old Athena Temple and the Hekatompedon (or 'Hundred-footer'), though both were dedicated to Athena, and it is safer to speak of the northern and southern temples. A big sixth century predecessor of the Parthenon has been restored hypothetically from fragments of architectural members and pedimental sculpture found here and there on the Acropolis. This had been demolished and was being replaced by a grander building of marble when the Persians sacked Athens in 480 and, to judge by the calcination of some of its remains, set fire to the scaffolding. From this unfinished Parthenon which was a little shorter and much narrower than its successor, several unfluted column drums (as well as triglyphs and metopes from another temple) are built conspicuously into the north wall of the Acropolis: they can be seen from the Agora, though the drums are visible also on the inside of the wall in a pit just east of the Erechtheum. To lessen the risk of damage it was normal practice with column drums that till they had been put in position they were not fluted except for a small strip at the bottom of the lowest drum, where it would have been difficult to avoid chipping the floor. A bottom drum so prepared stands on its side near the south-east corner of the present Parthenon.

It was thirty years before work began again and by then architectural taste had changed. The platform for the uncompleted temple was enlarged to the north and the old blocks of stones were re-used as far as was practicable, but the design was new, with end facades of eight columns. For an elaborate temple in the Doric style, however large, the normal number of columns at the ends was six: so, since the proportions of columns and the angle of the roof were fixed, a facade of eight columns was relatively lower and its pediment larger and more dominant. Perhaps the architects felt that in so prominent a situation a higher building would have been oppressive. Internally the sculptured frieze round the cella block is unique and the arrangements of this block are also unusual. The essential part of the Greek temple was the walled cella, with or without a surrounding colonnade, but its function was only to house the property and statue of the incumbent deity and not to accommodate congregational services, since these normally took place at the altar outside. So aesthetic effect was more important than utility in planning and designing, and indeed the Parthenon and other Greek temples can be regarded as abstract sculpture almost as much as architecture. Presumably the main reason for the back room here at the west was to reduce the cella to agreeable proportions, though it is not easy now to imagine the original effect. About 12 feet from the side and back walls there was a two-storey colonnade of small Doric columns and at the end of the central space a large base (now indicated by shallow blocks) supported Phidias's statue of Athena, a standing figure some 40 feet high with a surface of ivory and gold sheeting on a wooden core. The lighting, which came only through the eastern door, itself shaded by two rows of columns, must have been subdued and even, though not necessarily very dim, since the polished white marble of the floor and walls acted as a reflector. Of the quality of the statue, probably destroyed in a medieval fire in Constantinople, we know nothing directly; the ancients admired it without reserve, but it is kinder not even to look at the little souvenir replicas of Roman date. Of the paintings of the Byzantine church traces can be seen in the north-west corner of the back room.

Greek architecture is noted for its 'refinements', structurally unnecessary variations which were made deliberately. These refinements are most evident on the Parthenon, partly because it is an especially elaborate building and partly because they have been measured with exemplary precision. There is in fact hardly a single major line of the structure that is exactly vertical or horizontal. For instance the columns of the peristyle all tilt slightly inwards and on the long sides the line of the steps rises to a little more than 4 inches at the centre, as can be seen conveniently from the south-west corner. These refinements are usually considered as optical corrections to give an appearance of stability to the structure, and there seems no other explanation; if so, the modern eye is not educated to such subtleties.

The Athenians decorated the Parthenon, which was a show-piece of their imperial success, with an abundance of sculpture—in the pediments, on the metopes, and on the frieze round the outside of the cella in a position where it could not be seen properly. In all three places some fragments remain and others are on view in the Acropolis Museum, but the greater part of what survived was removed in 1801 by Lord Elgin and is now in the British Museum. As the most successful of collectors of works of art Elgin has often been reviled; but if his marbles should ever return to Greece, it would be ruinous to replace them on the Parthenon to be corroded by the air of modern Athens. The subjects of the metopes were the battles of Lapiths against Centaurs, Greeks against Amazons, Greeks against Trojans, and Gods against Giants; the frieze was inspired by the Panathenaic procession which made its way every four years from the Dipylon Gate, across the Agora, and up through the Propylaea to the Erechtheum, where a new robe was offered to the ancient idol of Athena; and the pediments represented, amid not very attentive deities, the birth of Athena and the contest for possession of Athens between Athena and Posidon (or, in the fashionable but unanglicised spelling, Poseidon). These last two subjects were appropriate to the temple and the procession at least to Athena, but those of the metopes had no particular relevance and, to judge from other temples, were chosen from the stock artistic repertory.

The Erechtheum   (*Plate* 5)

North of the Parthenon, just before the Erechtheum, excavation has exposed the plan of a fair-sized temple which the Persians ruined. The division of the cella block is like that of the later Erechtheum with a large room at the east and on the west an ante-room with two smaller rooms behind, but there was a colonnade all round. This temple dates to the sixth century B.C. and does not, as some say, go back to Mycenaean times.

The Erechtheum was built from about 421–406 B.C., had some alteration in the late first century B.C., duly became a church and later a dwelling, and was bombarded in 1826–7. Much of the exterior has been restored, though with the old materials. This part of the Acropolis contained a curious batch of shrines and holy places, but even piety hardly explains the irregularity of the porches nor does the inevitable suggestion of a curtailed plan make the problem simpler. The cella block is as usual rectangular, though its ground level is set 9 feet lower on the north and west, and it was divided internally to house Athena Polias at the east and the semi-divine king Erechtheus and other mythical personages at the west. There is a normal east porch, another larger porch overlaps the north side, a sort of dummy porch of partly engaged columns was set high up on the west end, and round the corner on the south side the Caryatid porch is too small to make good sense. The interior looks even more puzzling, but then it was gutted for later uses. The style of the building, which is all of marble, is Ionic of the finest quality and the unknown architect may be admired also for his management of the different levels. Inside the north porch a hole in the pavement still reveals the mark made by Zeus's thunderbolt and there is a corresponding hole in the roof above. The rich mouldings of the doorway are partly original and partly Roman replacements, which offer a useful exercise in detection, and the lining of the door is a Byzantine improvement. This porch had a sculptured frieze with figures of white marble pegged on to a background of dark stone—a rare alternative to painting the background—and another such frieze ran round the main building. The west facade, below which Athena's sacred olive tree has a modern successor, reproduces its Roman form: previously the columns had stood free in their upper parts. Of the Caryatids on the south one is a cast from the original acquired by the British Museum from Lord Elgin and another is modern. In Roman times these Caryatids were admired enough to be copied.

Other Buildings

It is easy to forget that in ancient times there was more than these buildings on the Acropolis. The Parthenon is now too starkly isolated in its eminence and the east front of the Propylaea may seem too large and grand for the bare expanse in front of it. Such false effects have been exaggerated by modern archaeology. Already in the sixth century B.C. the space within the walls was fairly closely covered with buildings and

Plate 2. Reconstructed view of the Acropolis of Athens from the Propylaea (G. P. Stevens).

statuary, as one realises in the Museum, although it exhibits only part of what survived the Persian sack; and Classical Athens was richer than Archaic. *Plate* 2 gives an impression, perhaps too uncluttered, of the prospect from the Propylaea around 400 B.C. In Medieval times most of these monuments disappeared, but the Acropolis was inhabited and even in the early nineteenth century travellers' drawings show the ancient ruins rising picturesquely out of a Turkish village. All this later accretion was cleared away after Greece became independent and in the search for buried antiquities the surface was stripped down to the rock.

The lesser buildings of the Classical Acropolis, like the major ones, kept more or less close to its edge, as probably had those of the Archaic period, known mainly from the pedimental sculptures in the Museum. On the right of the Propylaea as one enters was the sanctuary of Artemis Brauronia, a branch of the greater sanctuary at Brauron. It had a long Doric stoa backing on the Acropolis wall and another at right angles at the east, masking the view of the west end of the Parthenon nearly to the top of the columns. Beyond it a shed with a colonnade on the north

side stretched as far as the steps in front of the Parthenon; this should
be the Chalkotheke, so-called because bronze and other objects belong-
ing to Athena were stored there. On the other side of the Acropolis a
small building with a porch and yard was the house of the Arrephoroi,
small girls who served a spell as assistants to the priestess of Athena.
From here a stairway, which goes back to the Mycenaean period, led
outside the wall. The great altar of Athena stood south-east of the
Erechtheum, directly in front of the adjacent Archaic temple, and
towards the east end of the Acropolis there was a sanctuary of Zeus
Polieus and perhaps a precinct of Pandion. All these structures were of
the fifth century B.C., but hardly more than foundations of any remain.
Rather more survives of the round Ionic temple of Rome and Augustus,
put up east of the Parthenon in 27 B.C. and proof that Athenian builders
could still do good work. As for statues and carved and inscribed slabs,
they stood all over the free spaces of the Acropolis. Unluckily for us
there was no Persian destruction to save these monuments and very
few have survived, but cuttings in the rock (where they can be distinguished from later operations) and Pausanias's curiously selective
record give some idea of what once existed. The largest was Phidias's
bronze colossus of Athena Promachos, made about 450 B.C. and not less
than 30 feet high. Its base lies 40 yards east of the Propylaea, but the
statue itself has been destroyed, perhaps in A.D. 1203 in Constantinople.

The Acropolis Museum

The Museum, which is sunk discreetly near the south-east corner of the
Acropolis, possesses one of the great collections of Greek sculpture, for
Archaic unique though not comprehensive and for Classical exceptionally fine. Only the better or more interesting finds are exhibited, and
for these there is a good guide book in English. Greek sculpture began
rather before the middle of the seventh century B.C., but no example of
the early phase, which is conventionally named Daedalic, has been
found in Attica. Till the beginning of the fifth century two types of
statue were dominant, anyhow in European Greece—the naked standing
youth and the draped standing woman, both symmetrically frontal,
except that the youth regularly advances the left leg and the woman soon
takes a shorter pace forward and may move either arm across or in front
of the body. These Archaic types are usually described, by ancient words
but in a specialised modern sense, as 'kouros' and 'kore' (with plurals
'kouroi' and 'korai'). Till the Hellenistic period Greek statues had three

uses—as cult statues usually set up inside temples, as dedications to
celebrate public or private success or to pay a vow, and as monuments
on graves—and the same general type could serve for all purposes. The
statues that survive on the Acropolis are dedications, but the Greeks
too were susceptible to fashion and in Archaic Athens most dedicators
of a statue on the Acropolis chose a kore. The reason is not clear: the
kore does not represent Athena, who preferred a more military dress,
nor the dedicator, who where the inscription survives was male, and
perhaps the ancients themselves could not have given a rational explanation. Though there are kouroi on the Acropolis, including one of the
most important, the best series (from graves throughout Attica) is in
the National Museum and it is there that one can study the progress of
Archaic sculptors towards understanding of the structure and mechanism of the body. In the korai they were too often seduced by the charms
of drapery and coiffure, treated decoratively without much regard for
the practicalities of dressmaking or the relation of front and side view
of the hair style. Relief sculpture, of course, was from the beginning
freer in its movements, and in the Archaic period much of it is in technique as well as effect a sort of cut-out and slightly modelled drawing.
Here too poses were limited—the chest could be in front view, but
otherwise only profiles were permitted, and there is usually little depth
and a blank background. Pedimental sculpture, though the figures
came to be detached from the background, had the same rules as reliefs
but a more difficult problem of composition, since the field provided
by the gable (in which the figures were set) was a very low triangle. At
first snakes and other long-tailed creatures were favourites at the sides
or rows of human figures of diminishing size, but later the demand for
unity of subject and scale was met by lying and stooping poses. All this
sculpture was coloured, as can be seen in the Acropolis Museum better
than anywhere else.

In the first three rooms there are large parts of several big and small
pediments of limestone ('poros' to the archaeologists). These are thought
to date from the 570's to the 550's. No. 1 (in Room I) in very low relief
shows Heracles chopping off the heads of the monstrous Hydra, while
a crab sidles up to nip him—as often in Archaic art—and his horses
lower their heads to sniff and fit within the frame. In Room II No. 52,
the Olive Tree pediment, had Achilles waiting behind a fountain house
to ambush Troilus, while a little kore—roughly in the round—comes
out with her jar of water like the woman of the old-fashioned weather-
house. The representation of the setting—the building and the olive

tree engraved behind it—has parallels in vase painting, but in purely Greek sculpture did not establish itself till the Hellenistic period. We do not know how the corners were filled here. The pediment with the Introduction of Heracles into Olympus (Nos. 9+55) clumsily reduces the scale of the figures, though they were probably all human. These are small pediments, from buildings of the size of the treasuries at Olympia and Delphi. Much larger and bolder was the pediment which had Heracles struggling with Triton and a three-bodied monster at the two sides (No. 35); the centre was most likely the group of two lions killing a bull (No. 3 in Room III). The corresponding pediment may very well have had snakes (Nos. 37–40 in Room II) and a pair of couchant lions. Lastly in Room V we have most of Athena and of three Giants and also the hand of Zeus (since it holds a thunderbolt) from a big marble pediment of about 520 (No. 631). Here the figures were of one scale in poses justified by the subject, and the solution of the pedimental problem had been found. Later pediments can be seen at Olympia and in reconstructions. In these rooms of the Museum there are also some architectural members with traces of their original colouring.

The korai are in Rooms II to VI. The earliest, of about 560, is No. 593 in Room II, a headless block with drapery in flat vertical folds. About twenty years later comes No. 269 in Room IV, the 'Aphrodite of Lyons', so-called because the upper part is in Lyons and is represented here by a cast. In this statue a new fashion, borrowed from the Cyclades or Ionia and known as Ionic, allows the sculptor to vary the direction and depth of folds, enjoy the curves of buttocks and thighs while respectably avoiding outright nudity, and prettify face and hair. The new dress, which suggests a lighter material and has sleeves, is conventionally called the 'chiton' (to distinguish it from the heavier sleeveless 'peplos') and extra garments are usually worn on top. Most of the korai of the Acropolis wear these chitons. Some of the more exotic may be by sculptors trained in Cycladic workshops, such as No. 675 in Room IV; but the rest are Attic and often rather stolid, for example No. 681 in Room V, a big kore of about 520, perhaps by Antenor. The so-called Peplos kore (No. 679 in Room IV), which though carved about 530 still wears the old-fashioned dress, is more harmonious and also subtler in its modelling than appears at first sight. Subtler still is a small head No. 643 (Room IV), of the end of the century, which luckily has lost its body. The early fifth century brings a new strength and severity, very evident in the face of the kore which Euthydikos dedicated, though its

dress and hair wearily repeat the flashy formulas (Nos. 686+609 in
Room VI). The little figure No. 688 (Room VI) shows the next stage,
where the drapery too has been revised and heavy vertical folds match
the solidity of the features. Many of these korai (and other figures too)
stood on columns, for example that of Euthydikos. The metal spike
still protruding from the heads of some of them is the shaft of an um-
brella for protection from birds.

The most important of the kouroi of the Acropolis is the so-called
Critian Boy (No. 698 in Room VI), a work that should be only just
before 480 and illustrates admirably the transition to the Classical style.
Here the rigidity of the frontal pose is deliberately relaxed; the weight
is on the left leg and consequently the left hip is raised, and the head is
turned a little to the right. The Blond Head (No. 689) came from a
similarly relaxed statue: its stronger features look forward to the Apollo
of the West pediment of the Temple of Zeus at Olympia. There are
other types of Archaic statues. Of these the Moscophorus (or Calf-
carrier: No. 624 in Room II) is much admired, a work of around 560
representing a draped man bringing a calf to be sacrificed. The Rampin
rider (No. 590 in Room IV), which is a little later, breaks frontality by
turning his head, presumably so that the full view of a man's face should
not be obscured by the head of a horse. The sphinx (Nos. 630 and 632
in Rooms II and III), a monster of unknown and perhaps no religious
significance, was especially popular in the sixth century: it was often
put on grave monuments, but here must have been a dedication.

In the fifth century style developed quickly. About 460 the relief of
the 'Mourning Athena' (No. 695 in Room VI), more probably Athena
inspecting a boundary stone, still has the monotonous fall of Early
Classical drapery. The sculptures of the Parthenon (Rooms VII and
VIII) were made between 447 and 432 and go very much further: their
sequence is metopes, frieze, pediments. By the end of the century the
limits of elegant beauty were reached. No. 973 (Room VIII), a Victory
unfastening her sandal from the Nike Balustrade, exploits a pose which
is ugly in the nude but made attractive by the great hanging curves of
the skirt; and there is skilful alternation of deeply folded and clinging
drapery. The battered statue No. 1358 in Room IX is remarkable as
one of the few Classical originals whose sculptor is known: it must be
the Procne and Itys of Alcamenes made towards the end of the fifth
century.

The View from the Acropolis   (*Fig.* 3)

The view from Queen Amalia's Belvedere at the east end of the Acropolis is justly popular. From here and other parts of the wall almost all
of ancient and medieval Athens can be seen and measured against its
successor. Starting from the Monument of Philopappus, on the south
end of the hill opposite the Propylaea, the extended city wall of 479 B.C.
ran down to just beyond the Olympieum, there turned north to skirt
Syntagma Square (in front of the Old Palace) and Stadium Street to a
point two-thirds of the way to Omonia Square, and next swung round
through the Ceramicus to where the Observatory now stands on its
little peak; from there to the Philopappus Monument it followed the
further slopes of the hill. The space so enclosed was hardly more than a
mile across at its widest but contained the living city. Outside the gates
stretched the cemeteries. Two other walls, about four miles long, gave a
corridor to the Port of Piraeus and a third long wall diverged to the east
end of Phaleron Bay, providing shelter during invasion for refugees
from the country districts. In the early second century A.D. the Emperor
Hadrian extended the city wall on the east, but this was the limit of
expansion for ancient Athens. The new wall, run up around A.D. 280
after the Herulians had sacked the lower city, was more modest. Starting
from the Propylaea it cut down to the Stoa of Attalos, turned right past
the Library of Hadrian, and 200 yards further on returned to the east
end of the Acropolis. This circuit, about a quarter of a mile in diameter,
was usually sufficient for the petty medieval town.

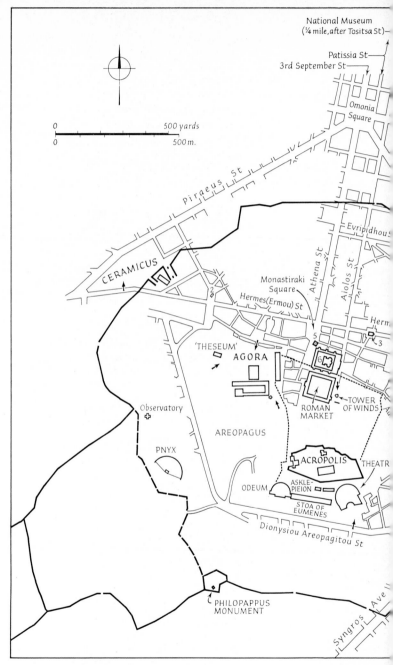

Fig. 3. Ancient Athens.

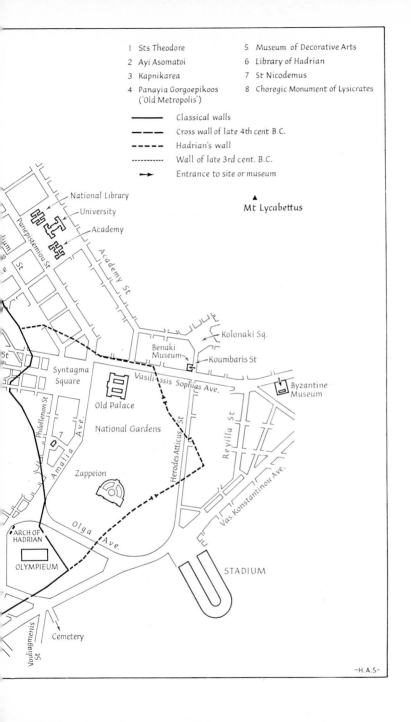

1 Sts Theodore
2 Ayi Asomatoi
3 Kapnikarea
4 Panayia Gorgoepikoos ('Old Metropolis')
5 Museum of Decorative Arts
6 Library of Hadrian
7 St Nicodemus
8 Choregic Monument of Lysicrates

——————— Classical walls
— — — — Cross wall of late 4th cent B.C.
- - - - - Hadrian's wall
·········· Wall of late 3rd cent. B.C.
——➤ Entrance to site or museum

▲ Mt Lycabettus

National Library
University
Academy

Panepistemiou St
St

Academy St

Kolonaki Sq.
Benaki Museum
Koumbaris St

Syntagma Square

Vasilissis Sophias Ave.

Byzantine Museum

Old Palace

Philellenon St

National Gardens

Herodes Atticus St

Reyilla St

Amalia Ave.

Zappeion

Vas. Konstantinou Ave.

ARCH OF HADRIAN

Olga Ave.

OLYMPIEUM

STADIUM

Vouliagmenis St

Cemetery

-H.A.S-

2 · Athens, the City

The Areopagus and the North Slope

On the north side of the entrance to the Acropolis a low hill stretches westwards, with its bare summit close to the car park. This is the Areopagus which gave its name to a Council, at one time the aristocratic governing body of Athens but from the 460's B.C. merely a court for homicide. St Paul preached here, though only faith can determine the exact spot. On the slopes below and stretching down to the Agora is the one domestic area of ancient Athens that has been excavated, a confusing network of ruins reaching back from Roman times to the fifth century B.C. The northern foot of the Acropolis itself is still more confusing. Here in caves and at other holy spots an excessive number of obscure cults were practised, most of which only the more imaginative students of ancient religion can elucidate.

The 'Theseum'   (*Plate* 3)

Below the Areopagus the Theseum stands on its little eminence. The name is mistaken, since the deity to whom it was dedicated was Hephaestus, the patron of craftsmen, and so archaeologists now prefer to speak of the Hephaesteum. It was begun soon after 450 B.C. by the architect who later built the temples of Ares (afterwards transferred to the Agora), of Posidon at Sunium and of Nemesis at Rhamnus—or so stylistic comparison suggests. Somehow this building survived the Herulian raid and the robbing of material for the new city wall and became a church that remained in Christian use till 1834. To meet Orthodox requirements the cella had doors cut in its west and side walls and an apse built into its porch, and at some time it lost its internal colonnade and was re-roofed with a barrel vault. From the standpoint of eternity roofing was the main weakness of the standard Greek temple; all the other parts were constructed of big blocks of stone, kept in place by gravity, but the roof was supported by timbers and these were liable to rot. The Theseum, though, was lucky in being repaired and not abandoned, and survives as the most complete of all sizable ancient

Plate 3. The 'Theseum' at Athens from the south-west (about 1752: J. Stuart and N. Revett).

temples. That it is not so much admired is probably because of the unfamiliar effect of its solid core and of the heavy shadows created by a roof. The modern eye still expects its ruins to be picturesque, with airy vistas between empty colonnades.

The Theseum is an excellent specimen of the Classical Doric temple, more instructive than the Parthenon because more normal. The external colonnade shows six columns at the ends and thirteen on the sides, the regular ratio for its time. In this, as in other proportions, Greek architectural taste kept moving; the sixth century preferred a ratio of six by sixteen columns, the fourth century six by eleven. The cella had a false back porch to match that in front, and though the east wall with the entrance door has disappeared, its position is given by the remains of bonding at the sides. Inside, a two-tier Doric colonnade was set close to the sides and back, enclosing a long base for the lost cult statues of Hephaestus and Athena. The architectural sculpture consisted of acroteria (figures set above the three angles of a pediment), pedimental groups and eighteen carved metopes (at the east end and for

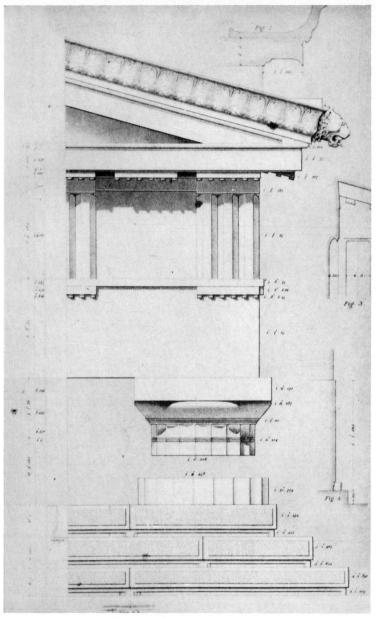

Plate 4. The Doric Order: Bassae, 450–420 B.C. (C. R. Cockerell).

two columns' distance down the sides). There were also carved friezes, abnormal in the Doric style, over each porch of the cella, that of the east even more abnormally carried across the corridor between the cella and the outer colonnade. Some fragments of this sculpture survive, either on the building or in the Agora Museum. The shrubbery round the temple is justified by Hellenistic flower pots found sunk in the ground there.

Till Roman times most buildings of architectural pretension in Greece and the West were designed in the Doric style (*Plate* 4), which varied little from one place to another, though as time went on the forms generally became lighter. The style seems to have been invented around the middle of the seventh century B.C., borrowing some structural details from timber construction but applying them decoratively and where they could not have been used in timber. A canonical system was established very quickly. The Doric building starts with a platform of three steps, resting on a level foundation—from some views the Theseum looks rather squat because the bottom step (which was not of marble) has broken away. The columns (or, if there is no colonnade, the walls) are set near the edge of the platform, have a curving taper upwards, and are channelled with twenty sharp-edged flutes. The capital consists of a spreading curved echinus surmounted by a low rectangular abacus. Next comes the architrave and frieze—the frieze composed of projecting three-barred triglyphs and flat squarish metopes, the architrave plain except for a band of drops ('guttae') just below each triglyph. The overhanging cornice above the frieze is also decorated with drops, and there is a raking cornice along the top of the gable. The low-pitched roof had a timber framework supporting big flat pantiles, normally of terracotta and slotted to fit over and be held in place by the one below; the side joins were protected by narrow cover tiles, similarly slotted, and wider cover tiles were used on the ridge. The last cover tile in each row often ended in an antefix, a decorative plate usually in the shape of a palmette, or alternatively the sima (or gutter) carried lion heads or other spouts so that the rain should be thrown clear of the platform. (There is a useful reconstruction of this type of roof at Corinth). Further decoration was provided by mouldings, paint and sculpture. Generally only those parts of a building were painted which appeared decorative rather than structural: so the ridges between the capital and the shaft were marked out in red, triglyphs were blue, bands and underside of cornice were picked out in contrasting colours, the back wall of the pediment was blue, appropriate patterns

Plate 5.
The Ionic Order:
north porch of the
Erechtheum at
Athens, late fifth
century B.C.
(J. Stuart and
N. Revett)

were applied to the cornices, and antefixes and spouts were painted too. Though the colour has usually vanished from stone, there are many terracotta pieces from cheaper buildings where it has survived. Sculpture was an optional extra.

Not only were the parts of the Doric building fixed, but also within limits the proportions between the parts. To take the most obvious effect, the size of the steps was related to the size of the whole, so that in a large temple they became too high for ordinary human legs and, as a compromise between the ideal and the necessary, a ramp was usually provided opposite the main door. One can indeed estimate the size of a Doric building from a single member, and might perhaps deduce from the steps the size of the temples on which the canon was established. Still, as time passed some of the proportions changed. For instance the spreading curve of the echinus of early capitals narrowed and straightened, till by Roman times it was often no more than a slanting collar; and columns tended to become slimmer and entablatures lower, so that in the Hellenistic period it was convenient to fill the space from one column to another with three instead of two sets of normally shaped triglyph and metope. The temple of Apollo at Corinth, the Theseum, and the temple at Nemea are good guides to the standards of the mid sixth, fifth and fourth centuries B.C.

With plans and elevations already so strictly regulated except in such rare buildings as the Propylaea and the Erechtheum, Greek architects turned to subtleties of detail. An early problem concerned the corner triglyph. The regular places for triglyphs were above the centre of columns and halfway between them and also there had to be a triglyph at the end of the frieze, but for stability the frieze needed to be centred on the columns, so that unless the width of the triglyph was exactly equal to the depth of the frieze the corner triglyph was bound to be eccentric. Since the Greeks chose to have relatively narrow triglyphs, those at the corners were centred outside their columns. To lessen this irregularity of spacing, which also affected the size of the metopes, various adjustments were explored; the neighbouring triglyphs could be shifted in sympathy, including that over the column next to the end, and the columns nearest the end could be set closer together. As for the columns, not only did they taper upwards, but the taper was curved, most strongly as it happens in the earlier work of Sicily and South Italy. Another early and normal irregularity is less easy to understand; the walls of the cella are not aligned with columns of the outer colonnade. There were also more refined experiments, such as the upward curve of the platform, the inward inclination of the axis of columns, and the curvature of all major horizontal lines. These refinements are known best in the Parthenon, but the Theseum had its share.

In Greece itself the Ionic style (*Plate 5*) was not so common as the Doric. It was more elegant and decorative, but less subtle. The columns, slimmer and often set further back from the steps, had moulded bases, normally twenty-four flat-edged flutes, and capitals composed of volutes. The architrave appeared to be in three players, toped by a moulded

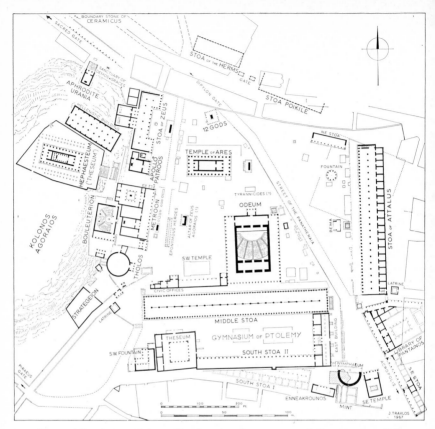

Fig. 4. The Agora, Athens (in the second century A.D.) *By courtesy of the American School of Classical Studies at Athens*

crown, and above it were dentils or a continuous frieze. Normally only the frieze carried sculpture. Since the standard Ionic capital differed in front and side views, there was a difficulty at the corner of a temple where two rows of columns met. This was solved very early by giving the capital two adjacent front faces with the shared volute projecting at 45°, and in the Hellenistic period a type of capital with four such fronts was common. As in Doric, capitals tended to contract, and the position of the eye of the volute in relation to the shaft of the column is a rough guide to date. The north porch of the Erechtheum is a good example of Classical Ionic, though the band of flowers and palmettes at the top of the shaft is an unusual enrichment.

The Agora (*Fig.* 4)

The Agora was the civic and commercial centre of a Greek city, and the Athenians presumably had one—perhaps near the entrance to the Acropolis—before the present site began to be developed about 600 B.C. in an area that had been used first for burials and then for houses. By 480, when the Persians destroyed Athens, there was a row of unimpressive buildings on the west side (at the foot of the rise on which the Theseum now stands) and a few other structures scattered round. During the fifth and fourth centuries new and grander edifices arose on the west, stoas bordered the north and south sides, and there was a large square court to the east. This court made way in the Hellenistic period for the much longer Stoa of Attalus, and a more complex block replaced the old South Stoa, but was destroyed in 86 B.C. In Roman times, when the market was on another site behind the Stoa of Attalus, large buildings were put up in the central space which before had been kept clear for stalls. Through all these changes the Agora was always irregular and in the main asymmetrical in its planning. The end came in A.D. 267 with the Herulian sack and the re-use of much of the stone from ruined buildings for the new city wall. Later, about 400, the authorities erected a 'gymnasium' (or high school) at the south and reconstructed a few minor buildings, but in the south-east corner of the old Agora a watermill was now allowed. In the sixth century the site was deserted once more, and when re-occupied in the tenth century it was with houses, the successors of which were demolished by the American excavation. This excavation has not produced impressive ruins or many notable objects of art, but it is the first satisfactory exploration of a large Greek site. Careful digging has been followed—most unusually—by meticulous sorting and cataloguing of the finds, study, publication, and presentation to the visitor. The example of the Agora has prodded the consciences of Classical archaeologists a little, though not enough.

Some of the barrenness of the ruins has been concealed by skilful landscape gardening, but it needs imagination or sentiment to make them enjoyable and those who want a detailed description should get the excellent guide book to the site and museum. The Classical buildings along the west side below the Theseum, parallel to one another but not in alignment, were mostly public offices. At the south the Tholos—a word used in ancient Greek for round buildings but not tombs—was the office of the duty officers. About 20 yards in front of it is a boundary stone of the Agora, so inscribed, set up about 500 B.C.

Next to the Tholos was the Council House (Bouleuterion) and the
Metroon (or sanctuary of the Mother of the Gods) where archives were
kept. After a gap to give access to the Theseum there were a small
temple, a very small temple and the Stoa of Zeus, a Doric building with
wings projecting forward and so providing another triglyph problem,
the more intractable one of an inner corner. In front of all this range is a
well built rainwater drain of the early fifth century B.C., and several
other such drains can be seen around the excavated area. There were
more stoas beyond the electric railway. In the central space opposite the
Stoa of Zeus the fenced-in Altar of the Twelve Gods counted as the
centre of Athens for measuring distances by road. South of the Altar
in the position now marked by a rectangle of broken stones was the
temple of Ares, built probably in Acharnae (8 miles to the north) about
the same time as the Theseum and moved to the Agora in the late
first century B.C., when country towns and villages were giving way to
large estates. The colossal figures of a Giant and two Tritons acted as
piers in the portico of the Odeum when it was rebuilt in the mid second
century A.D. and were re-used for the gymnasium of 400. To the south-
west, set up against the wall of a public office, there are two slabs with
roof tiles carved on them as official standards; and beyond them and
abutting on the rectangular enclosure now thought to be the genuine
Theseum, a 'klepsydra' or water-clock was installed in the fourth century
B.C. It consisted of a waterproofed rectangular tank with a metal pipe as
outlet and the passage of time was measured by a graduated scale
mounted on a float. The tank and outlet survive. Another mechanical
appliance is the water-mill of the fifth century A.D. just south of the
Stoa of Attalus; there remain a stretch of the water channel and the pit
for the overshot wheel. Near-by is a piece of the city wall of the third
century A.D., showing nakedly at the back how such late fortifications
were constructed. The road in front is the Panathenaic Way, the route
of the great procession. It was about 30 feet wide, partly gravelled and
partly paved, and led from the Dipylon Gate obliquely across the Agora
and round between the Areopagus and the Acropolis to below the
Propylaea. On the west side of the road the little Byzantine church of
the Holy Apostles has been restored to its original eleventh century
form. It is fair in quality, but abnormal in plan—cross in square with
an apse at the end of each arm. though the symmetry is partly concealed
at the west by the narthex or vestibule. Pierced marble sheets in
windows were regular till glazing came into general use, and the Cufic
decoration outside—Arabic or pseudo-Arabic letters in brickwork—

seems to be especially characteristic of the early and middle eleventh century.

The Stoa of Attalus on the east side of the Agora was built in the mid second century B.C. by Attalus II, king of Pergamum in Asia Minor and an alumnus of what might be called the university of ancient Athens. After the destruction of A.D. 267 its ruins were incorporated in the new city wall and so preserved enough to allow a complete restoration on paper. The new stoa, constructed by the Americans in 1953-6 as museum, store and offices for the excavation, is a fairly accurate replica of the original, but has of course been criticised. Admittedly its style is poor, but that is the fault of the mid Hellenistic period, not of the restorers, and anyhow some large building was needed for the finds, the site chosen was as inoffensive as any, this was the only suitable ruin that could be restored convincingly, and a restoration of this sort teaches even the specialist more about the nature of a building than models or architects' drawings. The standard stoa is a long hall with an open colonnade at the front, a more widely spaced internal colonnade, and sometimes lock-up rooms for shops, offices, or taverns at the back. Most stoas were one storey high, but some (like this) had an upper floor. In the lower storey, as often, the outer colonnade was Doric and the inner —to get extra height—Ionic. The squat upper storey has Ionic outside, but the 'palm' capitals inside are a Hellenistic innovation that never became popular in this simple form. With its wide sheltered promenades the Stoa of Attalus is an admirable place for passing time in, especially on a hot summer day, and one can examine in comfort the shifting effects of light and shadow across the front of the Theseum.

Only a small selection of the finds from the excavation are on show in the Museum. Of the sculpture, spaced out easily in the lower promenade, S.1882, probably an Aphrodite of around 420 B.C., has admirably swirling drapery; rather later the acroterion, S.182, exploits transparency; and the fragments of two figures of Nike, probably acroteria from the Stoa of Zeus (S.312 and 373), show the development towards exuberance around 400 B.C. The later works are more interesting than enjoyable. The body of a draped male (S.657) has the distinction of being the latest of ancient statues found in Athens; it is of the fifth century A.D. and has unlearnt all the principles of Classical style. When one considers how much sculpture there was once in the Agora and how little is left, it is easy to understand why the latest structures on Greek sites are so often lime kilns.

Some of the rooms behind contain pottery and other small objects,

well labelled and unusually instructive about the habits and processes of
ancient life. Examples are the miniature terracotta boots of the ninth
century B.C. (Case 18), a child's chamber pot of the early sixth century
B.C. properly decorated with animals (Case 35), and an assortment of
ordinary household ware (Cases 37, 39, 41). Commercial wine jars are
displayed in a separate room. The public antiquities include a small
portable 'klepsydra', limiting the length of speeches in the law-courts,
jurors' ballots and tickets and a machine for picking jurors (Cases 27
and 28)—for the Athenians regarded the appointment of officials by lot
as an essential of democratic government. There are also various public
weights and measures (Case 26) and potsherds (or 'ostraka') on which
are scratched the name of a candidate for 'ostracism', a constitutional
device used occasionally in fifth century Athens for voting some trouble-
some politician into exile for ten years (Case 38). Other curiosities are
part of the mould for a bronze kouros apparently as early as the mid
sixth century B.C. (Case 23) and a bronze shield inscribed as taken from
the Spartans at Pylos in 425 B.C. (Case 34). In the last of the row of
rooms, beyond the modern W.Cs., well linings, water pipes, roof tiles,
a bath tub and braziers are displayed and explained. In the promenade
upstairs there are more pieces of sculpture and some architectural
models.

The Ceramicus

The Ceramicus or Kerameikos (depending on whether one prefers an
Anglicised or transliterated version) lay north-west of the Agora. Here
excavation has been carried on by the Greeks and the Germans and the
site is open to visitors by a gate off the modern Hermes Street. The name
Ceramicus means potters' quarter, but the part of the district outside
the city wall of the fifth century B.C. was used for burials from the
twelfth or eleventh century B.C. till the fifth century A.D., when Christianity established itself, and by the Classical period this was the most
distinguished of Athenian cemeteries, stretching out along the roads to
Eleusis, the Academy and Piraeus. The rise in the level of the ground,
from detritus or dumping, allowed new graves to be put above earlier
ones and at least twice—in 479 and 338 B.C.—there was an extensive
clearance of its monuments, when the Athenians needed stone urgently
for their city wall. Archaeologists and others tend to exaggerate the
importance of burials, which often provide good specimens of pottery
and other objects of use or ornament but are unreliable guides to reli-

gious belief. Certainly in ancient Athens the alternation of burning and inhuming corpses was not connected with changes of creed, anyhow after the eighth century B.C., and offerings were put in graves even though there was no hope of an effective after-life. The early graves in the Ceramicus were marked (if at all) by a rough stone or, in the eighth and seventh centuries, by a large pot. The carving or painting of monuments began around 600 and soon became regular, though a limit on expenditure was imposed about 317 B.C. and presumably—to judge by the lack of finds—there had been a similar restriction from the end of the sixth to the middle of the fifth century B.C. One may imagine private graves of the Classical Athenians grouped in terraced family plots with cypresses and shrubs planted round and the busy highway passing through the middle. Some of these monuments have been re-erected or replaced by casts. Near the city wall a few useful structures have been found—a public hot bath of about 400 B.C. and several kilns of the next two centuries.

At the east end of the site there is a stretch of city wall with two gates —the Dipylon Gate with its double doorway and the smaller Sacred Gate, used for the procession to Eleusis. The wall was built first in 479 B.C. and from time to time repaired or reconstructed, as can be observed in the successive masonry bases, each higher than the last, to the south of the gates. Between the gates on the inside stood the Pompeion, from which the Panathenaic procession started. It was built early in the fourth century, destroyed in 86 B.C. rebuilt at a higher level in the second century A.D. and destroyed again in 267.

The Museum has some good grave monuments, though the National Museum has more, and an archaeologically important series of Protogeometric and Geometric pottery. A pair of terracotta cocks of the middle of the eighth century B.C. are the earliest evidence for poultry in Europe.

The Roman Market

The Roman Market begins about a hundred yards east of the Agora and has been partly excavated by the Greeks. Its surroundings and air of neglect give the site a melancholy charm, lost by other Athenian ruins. In contrast with the Greek Agora the Roman Market, laid out in the last years of the first century B.C., was symmetrical in plan, a large open rectangle with colonnades on all four sides and a principal entrance in the centre of the east end. This entrance is a double Doric porch, well preserved and of an architectural purity unexpected in its period. At the opposite end another porch, off centre and not in strict alignment, led up to the Tower of the Winds. The mosque to the north is of the later fifteenth century; it has been shorn of its minaret and is now an archaeological repository. Near the ticket gate one can examine an ancient public lavatory, of Roman type and date.

The Tower of the Winds

The Tower of the Winds or, to use its original name, the Horologion of Andronikos was constructed by Andronikos in the early or middle first century B.C. to serve as a chronometer. It is a well preserved octagon with pyramidal roof of marble slabs carved to imitate tiles and originally surmounted by a bronze weather-cock in the shape of a Triton. At the top of the walls there are clumsy carvings of the eight winds with scorings for sun-dials below them. Inside there was an elaborate water-clock to which the puzzling channels belong, as does the round reservoir attached outside on the south. In the later Middle Ages, when the Athenians—presumably to satisfy visitors—discovered names for the surviving relics of their misty past, the Horologion became the School or Tomb of Socrates. Under the Turks the Dervishes took over and protected it.

The Library of Hadrian

The Library and Stoa of Hadrian stood parallel to the Roman Market a little to its north. The block was built around A.D. 130 and its massive enclosing wall incorporated in the fortifications of the fourth century. The west end with the entrance was faced with a row of Corinthian columns. Inside there was a rectangular court surrounded by colonnades and of about the same size as the Market. At the east end a higher building with two or three floors or galleries housed the library. In the middle of the court Hadrian's builders put a long ornamental pool, but early in the fifth century this was replaced by a complicated edifice of roughly quatrefoil plan, notable in the history of early Christian architecture. It was altered or rebuilt a hundred years or so later to conform to the basilical plan then popular for churches. Much of the rusticated outer wall of the enclosure survives on the north and east and half the wall and outer columns on the west. Their effect is still impressive, particularly as one comes up from Monastiraki Square past the mosque that now houses the Museum of Decorative Arts.

The Choregic Monument of Lysicrates

The Choregic Monument of Lysicrates, a quarter of a mile south-east of the Tower of the Winds and close to the Theatre of Dionysus, is an elegant little folly. Its only function was to support the tripod won by Lysicrates in 334 B.C. as financial backer of one of the companies which competed in the annual dramatic contests in the near-by Theatre. This backing was one of the duties that Athenian law imposed on the rich and the prize of a tripod was in effect honorary, since it was the rule that these useless objects were set up as dedications in a sanctuary or other public place. There are traces of several choregic monuments near that of Lysicrates and elsewhere round the Theatre, and why this one survived is a puzzle. It was helped perhaps by the curvature of much of its masonry, which was less convenient for re-use than squared blocks. That incidentally is why in general the columns of temples have been robbed much less than cella walls. In the late Middle Ages the Monument of Lysicrates was called the Lantern of Demosthenes and in 1669 it was built into the Capucin monastery as an alcove in their library. Here at a later date Byron is said to have written stanzas of his 'Childe Harold', and indeed as a guest of the monks he is not likely to have overlooked so romantic an opportunity. The structure, which has had a little repair, is remarkably complete. It is composed of a tall square pedestal, a taller drum with six attached columns and frieze, and a conical roof topped by an acanthus finial. On the upper surface of the finial are cuttings to hold a bronze tripod, which has of course been looted: it should be imagined as a shallow bowl on three long straight legs. The roof, a single piece of marble, has leaf-shaped tiles carved on it; the sculptured frieze shows Dionysus transforming the pirates into dolphins; and the columns have Corinthian capitals, the only feature in which the Corinthian order differs from the Ionic. This is the first known use of a Corinthian capital on the outside of a building, though it had appeared internally towards the end of the fifth century, and it remained uncommon and experimental for another three centuries, till Augustus's architects designed and established a standard form in Rome.

The South Slope

The South Slope of the Acropolis has more sentimental than aesthetic delights. At the east is the *Theatre of Dionysus*, the place but not the structure in which the great Attic tragedies were first produced. The site was being used for dramatic performances by the beginning of the fifth century B.C. and before its end there was beyond the circular orchestra (or dancing floor) a stone building serving as the back of the stage, but the auditorium was no more than the terraced hillside with some temporary seating. Around 340 B.C. the auditorium was re-modelled in stone and now had perhaps 17,000 places, and the stage was rebuilt more grandly. Some time later, to suit Hellenistic production, the stage was raised and during the first century B.C. the chairs of honour in the front row were provided, perhaps copying fourth-century predecessors. In the middle of the first century A.D. and again a century or more later the stage was pushed forward, encroaching on the orchestra; the marble floor of the orchestra belongs to the first, the sculpture on the front wall of the stage to the second of these reconstructions. The cutting down of this sculpture was perpetrated still later, when the orchestra was waterproofed for aquatic spectacles. Backing on the stage building was a stoa and in front of this two temples and an altar of Dionysus. The two Corinthian columns above the Theatre were more choregic monuments which once supported their tripods.

West of the Theatre, close to the Acropolis rock, are the scanty remains of the *Asklepieion*. Asklepios was a medical deity, who made his reputation at Epidaurus and gained wider recognition in the late fifth century B.C. The sanctuary contained an altar, two springs, temples and stoas, one of which was used by patients as a dormitory where they consulted the god in dreams. In the fifth century A.D. Christianity took over the practice, and the ruins of a basilical church are with cisterns of various dates the most easily intelligible structures on the site.

Below the Asklepieion a stoa nearly 180 yards long stretched most of the way from the Theatre to the Odeum. This is thought to be the *Stoa of Eumenes II*, who was king of Pergamum in the first half of the second century B.C. The conspicuous arcade was a retaining wall, originally concealed by the back wall of the stoa, which had in front of it the usual inner and outer colonnades. There was probably a second storey.

The *Odeum of Herodes Atticus*, donated by this Herodes in the middle of the second century A.D., has survived so well because in the eleventh century it was incorporated in the fortifications. It has been renovated in recent years and is again in use. Except that the auditorium is set into the hillside instead of being built up from level ground, the Odeum is a typical Roman theatre with semi-circular auditorium and, joining it and of equal height, an ornate wall backing the tallish stage. The standard Greek theatre used a natural slope, as far as was practicable, for its auditorium, which extended round the circular orchestra for more than a semi-circle, and the stage building beyond the orchestra was low and detached. Herodes Atticus was the last of the great benefactors and his name recurs at many ancient sites. Gifted, well educated and excessively rich he married into the Emperor's family, held the consulship at Rome and maintained a dubiously cultural circle in his mansion at Marathon. The Odeum was a memorial to his wife, whose tomb is on the Appian Way at Rome. Most of his buildings are showily vulgar.

The Olympieum and its Vicinity

It is difficult to miss the Arch of Hadrian and the Olympieum, which stand about a quarter of a mile to the east of the Acropolis, across the main road. The Arch is a slender gateway, two storeys high, of around A.D. 130 and commemorates in inscriptions Hadrian's enlargement of the circuit of Athens. Beyond it is the precinct of Olympian Zeus with a few gigantic columns isolated in the bare open space. The temple, one of the largest built by the ancients, was begun and abandoned in the late sixth century B.C. Around 170 B.C. Antiochus IV, king of Syria, made a new start, changing the order from Doric to Corinthian, but he died when building was half done; after capturing Athens in 86 B.C. Sulla had some of the columns and capitals removed to Rome as models for the local architects. The temple was completed by Hadrian around A.D. 130. In the Middle Ages, when that form of asceticism became fashionable, a stylite took up his station on a piece of architrave above two of the columns. Some column drums from the original undertaking are to be seen in a pit on the north of the precinct.

The Stadium is further east, across the now buried river Ilissus. When first laid out about 330 B.C., it was a natural hollow between two low hills, stopped at the far end by an embankment. Herodes Atticus put in marble seats in A.D. 140–4, and Averoff paid for the restoration between 1895 and 1906. The effect is too grand to be Greek.

The Pnyx

The ridge opposite the Propylaea offers a fine view of the Acropolis, but its own remains are less spectacular. Along or just over the crest are the lowest courses of a cross-wall, built at the end of the fourth century B.C., when the Long Walls to the Piraeus were no longer effective. The peak at the south end is crowned with the Monument of Philopappus, an

elaborate mausoleum of the early second century A.D., improved
aesthetically by the battering it has taken. Towards the north is the
Pnyx, the meeting place of the sovereign Assembly, to which in the great
period of Athenian democracy all citizens belonged. It was a sort of
open theatre with instead of a stage a platform from which speakers
addressed the Assembly. In its earliest form, about 500 B.C., the
auditorium faced downhill, but in 404–3 a big embankment was put up
hastily at the bottom and the arrangements were reversed. After the
middle of the fourth century B.C. improvements were begun but not
completed, presumably because the remodelled Theatre of Dionysus
(which unlike the Pnyx had seats) was a more convenient place for
meetings.

Neoclassical Buildings

Some modern buildings deserve archaeological notice at this point.
The University and the Academy, both by Hansen, revive the spirit of
Herodes Atticus, while the Old Palace (facing Syntagma Square) is a
more stolid essay by Gärtner in Classicism. The Palace and the
University were built around 1840, the Academy twenty years later.

Byzantine Churches

In the early Christian period Athens was too much interested in main-
taining Pagan culture, of which it was the most hallowed seat, to accept
the new religion readily. So it neglected to insure its future with attractive saints or relics, and besides Greece was becoming more and more a
backward province and Athens a provincial town. It is then not surprising that the Medieval churches of the city are mediocre as well as small.
No example survives of the early basilical type, which was the standard
of the fourth and fifth centuries A.D., nor are there any lucid ruins of one
in Athens, so that it is better to wait for Brauron (*Fig.* 7) or Corinth.
The earliest remaining Athenian churches are of the centralised type
that is considered specifically Byzantine. This type, which first found
Christian use in martyrs' tombs, was taken over for churches in the
fifth century and soon became popular. Its commonest versions (*Plate* 9
and *Fig.* 16) were cruciform in plan with a dome rising on a drum above
the crossing; the arms were short and tended to be equal in length, the
corners between the arms were often filled with lower rooms (giving the
'cross in square' or 'quincunx' plan), the east arm ended in an apse, and

there was a narthex or closed vestibule across the west end. This basic plan could be elaborated with more apses and domes. Since each part of the church was roofed separately, the elevation in its upper part offered an interesting and interrupted series of levels. One thinks of brick as the characteristic Byzantine material, but stone was used too and in Greece from the beginning of the eleventh century (when it was developing a school of its own) there was a taste for the cloisonné technique, in which each block of stone is framed by bricks. Though additions and alterations have been made to many of the surviving specimens of the centralised church, it is not hard to comprehend their original exterior form, but inside they have generally suffered serious damage or renovation and the reconstructed interior in the Byzantine Museum is very helpful. In size these centralised churches are mostly very small, since Orthodox ritual—once properly codified—did not allow the laity much part in services nor had the monasteries now large establishments of clergy. Still what was lost in size was made up in number; when the Turks came there are said to have been about 150 churches in Athens for a not very wealthy population of perhaps 10,000.

The earliest remaining churches in Athens are thought to be of the eleventh century, though the dating of Middle Byzantine architecture is not yet secure. The largest of them (but disastrously restored) is *St Nicodemus* in Philhellenon Street, the finest the *Saints Theodore* in Klavthmonos Square (to the south of Stadium Street), the quaintest with its re-use of older carved blocks the *Panayia Gorgoepikoos* (or 'Old Metropolis') south of Hermes Street. Lower down Hermes Street are *Kapnikarea*—in spite of later accretions a harmonious little building— and *Ayi Asomatoi*, both of the twelfth century. *Holy Apostles* on the Agora site near-by, of the eleventh century, is untypical in its plan. Most of these churches now look too squat because of the rise in street level, a normal process before roads were properly surfaced.

There are more impressive churches from monasteries founded in the countryside round Athens, though now on its outskirts. *Kaisariani* (*Plate* 6), at the foot of Hymettus on the road which goes to the top of the mountain, is idyllic. The present church was built in the twelfth century, though the narthex is of the seventeenth and the annexed chapel and monastic buildings (recently restored) go back to the sixteenth. Inside the church four re-used Roman columns support the dome, and the wall paintings which are of the Turkish period have their admirers. The monastery was deserted in the eighteenth century. Another little monastery, also deserted and enclosed by a high wall, nestles on the steep hillside further up the road. This is *Asteri*, of much the same date both for the structure and the paintings of the church, but because of its setting more austere in effect. Unlike Kaisariani it is usually shut. There are several more Medieval monasteries along the flank of Hymettus. At the north end of Tourkovouni the 'Beautiful Church'—*Omorphi Ekklesia*—is a pleasant, presumably monastic building of the twelfth or thirteenth century; the narthex is later. It has remains of paintings of the fourteenth century. One can reach Omorphi Ekklesia by way of Filothei, turning off the main road to Kifisia and passing the arches of Hadrian's aqueduct, or from the Patissia road turning off through Galatsi.

Daphni is in a different class, larger in size and metropolitan in style. It stands on the saddle between Athens and Eleusis, to the left of the main road. Here there was once a sanctuary of Apollo, which was replaced by a fortified monastery probably in the sixth century. The existing church (except for the outer porch) was built in the late eleventh century, occupied from 1211 to 1458 by Cistercians, left to decay in the late eighteenth century when the monks moved out, and restored with creditable care at various times since the 1890's. The enclosing wall goes back to the first monastery, though the battlements are Frankish; the domestic buildings are of the Turkish period; and there are excavated foundations of various dates. The design of the church is sophisticated, giving more importance to the central area, which is spanned by a wide and relatively low dome. In most Middle Byzantine churches in Greece the dome is supported by arches and pendentives on four columns or piers, but here there are eight supports, with broader arches across the four arms and narrower squinches between them, and the pendentives (now eight) are small. The intended effect of spaciousness has, though, been exaggerated by the loss of the furnishings and of the marble slabs and veneering of the floor and lower parts of the wall.

The mosaics of the upper part of the interior are in part restored, but still of remarkable quality. Their arrangement conforms to Orthodox regulations, though through damage they are no longer a complete set. In the centre of the dome—since one always begins at the top—Christ, the Lord of All ('Pantokrator'), looks down on the visitor. Round his bust, at a lower level, stand the Prophets. Below come the incidents celebrated by the great festivals of the Church. The Annunciation, the Nativity, the Baptism and the Transfiguration are exhibited on the squinches, the Entry into Jerusalem, the Crucifixion, the Descent into Hell and the Incredulity of Thomas in the side bays beneath the Raising

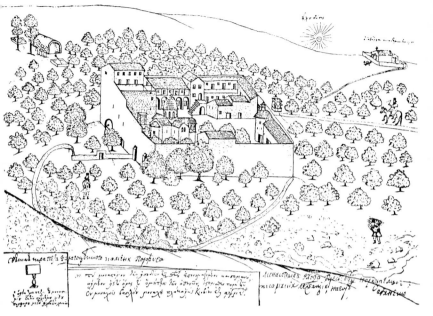

Plate 6. The Monastery of Kaisariani near Athens (V. G. Barsky, 1745).

of Lazarus, the Birth of the Virgin, the Adoration of the Magi and the Presentation in the Temple. In the chancel the Virgin and Child occupy the apse, flanked by the Archangels Michael and Gabriel. Opposite, over the main doorway, is the Dormition of the Virgin. Below the level of the arches and in the narthex there were more scenes from the Lives of Jesus and the Virgin and the inferior spaces still available were filled by saints and martyrs. Byzantine mosaics are generally much more admired than the Greek and Roman mosaics from which they are derived. The first figured mosaics appeared in the fifth century B.C. and were more or less linear drawings done in black and white pebbles; there are examples in the museums of Corinth and Sicyon. By the end of the third century B.C. the small coloured cubes called tesseras had replaced pebbles and designs were based on the advanced illusionist painting of the time, with effects about as satisfactory as those of Gobelin tapestries. In the Roman period a stiffness of style often appears with an increase in frontal views and a reduction of the background to conventional symbols, but it is not clear how far this was from incompetence or a positive change of vision. The tendency continued in Byzantine art and was re-interpreted by religious dogma; but though there was a new sublety in the use of the formulas, especially in the application of designs to curved surfaces, the modelling of faces and drapery still showed its Hellenistic origin and since specimens of the ancient style survived (particularly in illustrations in manuscript books) Byzantine artists were liable at any time to turn back to the past, so that for instance the mosaics of Daphni could be both more Hellenistic and later than those of Holy Luke's. This makes it difficult or impossible to trace a tidy development in Byzantine mosaics or even to define the general standard at any single time. Byzantine painting had a similar relation to the past, though because its technique was freer and the art was in greater demand there was more deliberate experiment as well as provincial aberration. At Daphni the paintings, which appear faintly on the lower parts of the walls, are poor late work, covering the bare patches where the marble cladding had been removed.

The now roofless outer porch (or 'exonarthex'), which was added by the Cistercians, is more amusing than appropriate. On its west front the arches were pointed according to the contemporary Western but not Byzantine style, and at its south end the Ionic columns and capitals are ancient pieces re-used. Other ancient blocks, recognisable by their size, were built into the outer walls of the church and in some places are arranged to form a Christian cross.

3 · Athens, the Museums

The archaeological museums of Athens are numerous and important. There are the National Museum, the Museums of the Acropolis, the Agora and the Ceramicus (these three already described), the Byzantine Museum, the Benaki Museum, and the Museum of Decorative Arts. Of these the most important are the National Museum, the Acropolis Museum and the Byzantine Museum.

The National Museum   (*Fig. 5*)

The National Museum, extended and modernised since the last war, houses finds from Attica (excepting generally the Acropolis, the Agora, the Ceramicus, Piraeus, Brauron and Eleusis) and has gathered objects from other parts of Greece where at the time there was no adequate museum or the local authorities could not resist the acquisitiveness of Athens. Though it has the biggest collection of Greek art in the world, this collection is not fully representative—fortunately so for visitors or they would be even more overfaced.

PREHISTORIC COLLECTION

The Prehistoric collection is straight ahead as one enters the Museum. The main hall contains Mycenaean finds, the left side gallery earlier finds mostly from the Greek mainland, and the right side gallery finds from the Cyclades. A good guide book in English can be bought at the counter.

The Myceanaean hall displays most of the spectacular objects of Mycenaean art discovered throughout Greece, particularly those from the two sets of shaft graves at Mycenae, and though items found together have usually been kept together the effect is that of a treasure house rather than an explanatory series. Mycenaean art began early in the sixteenth century B.C. in frank imitation of the older Minoan art of Crete, and apparently some Cretan artists too were imported by

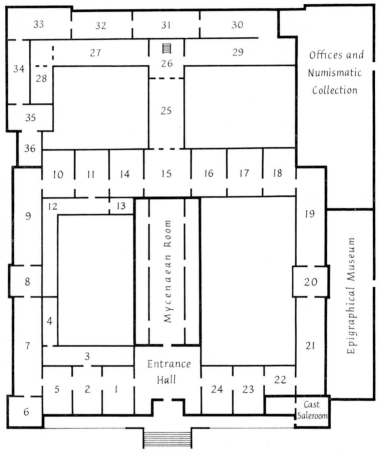

Fig. 5. The National Museum, Athens: ground floor. The numbering of the rooms is not official. The Vase Collection is reached by the stairway in Room 26.

Mycenaean patrons. Though very soon a different range of subjects became established, the divergence in style was due as much to lesser sensitivity as to any positive new direction. The best work was done in valuable materials and on a small scale—inlaid and embossed metalwork, carved ivories and engraved seals; but wall paintings though often attractive are mediocre, large sculpture is rare and poor, pottery is technically well made but ranks as a craft rather than an art, and not even that can be said of the careless little terracotta figurines. Most of these arts depended on the wants of the palaces and disappeared with them at the end of the thirteenth century, and though pottery survived its originally natural forms became unrecognisably abstract and the earlier uniformity of the Mycenaean style disintegrated into local schools.

Chronologically one might begin the tour of the collection with the contents of the shaft graves of Circle B at Mycenae (in Cases 5 and 6, on the left just before the middle door); their date is late seventeenth and early sixteenth century. The rock crystal saucer in the form of a duck (No. 8638) and the amethyst seal (No. 8708) should not be missed. The shaft graves of Circle A, which Schliemann found, are rather later and much richer, and their contents are set out nearer the entrance in and around Cases 3–4, 22–25 and 27–29. Here the gold rings of Case 27 (Nos. 240–1) are easily overlooked. In Case 30 the ivory group of two females and a boy (No. 7711) from the citadel of Mycenae is an exceptional work hardly later than the early fourteenth century. The so-called Warrior Vase (No. 1426) of the twelfth century is also exceptional, since human figures are unusual on Mycenaean pottery, but the drawing is clumsy. The partial reconstruction of the two engaged columns from the Treasury of Atreus is helpful after a visit to Mycenae. As for the wall paintings, it is difficult to see a development in style since most are late —of the fourteenth or thirteenth century—and all are fragmentary: the restorations are not reliable and should be discounted. Case 9, on the left beyond the middle door, offers tablets from Pylos inscribed in the Linear B script and using an early dialect of Greek; they were ephemeral records of the palace, noted on raw clay, and have survived only by the chance that the palace was burnt and these tablets fired hard. Further on in the middle of the hall are the two gold cups from Vaphio near Sparta (Nos. 1758–9), probably Cretan work of the fifteenth century and admirable examples of the style the Mycenaeans copied.

In the gallery on the left the earlier finds from the Greek mainland make a poor showing. The fullest series is from Thessaly and includes some Mycenaean objects, and there is a little from Troy and Lemnos too. The Cycladic gallery on the other side is more interesting. 'Cycladic' is a term used conventionally of the Bronze Age culture of the central and western islands of the Aegean, a culture that is not well understood but evidently had a distinctive character in its Early period, though afterwards it was affected strongly by Minoan and then Mycenaean. The most remarkable exhibits are the Early Cycladic 'idols' marble figurines found in graves and not made to stand up, so that they probably do not represent deities. These idols were very much to the taste of the 1920's and forgeries became frequent, though most of the National Museum's holdings are certified by excavation.

SCULPTURE COLLECTION

The sculpture collection opens off the left side of the entrance hall and as there are more than twenty rooms it is as well to be selective when passing through. The first seven rooms contain Archaic sculpture, from the middle of the seventh century to 480 B.C. and illustrate the development of the naked male statue (the 'kouros'), though for its draped female counterpart (the 'kore') one must go to the Acropolis Museum. In Room 1 the most prominent exhibit is the so-called Dipylon amphora, an outsize terracotta jar made about 750 B.C. as a monument on a grave in the Ceramicus cemetery (near the Dipylon Gate); it is the classic example of the mature Attic Geometric style and its painter through his severely logical analysis of the human figure is the first European artist whose personality is discernible. The sculpture begins a century later. A battered and very simple female figure dedicated in Delos by Nikandre (No. 1) is our earliest sizable Greek statue, with shallow triangular face and long and hardly modelled body; its date is about 650. The relief from Mycenae (No. 2866) is a slightly later and less austere expression of the same pioneering phase, the so-called Daedalic style. In Room 2 the big kouros from Sunium (No. 2720) is eccentric Attic work of around 600; its face has been restored wrongly and must have been more like that of the Dipylon head (No. 3372) which belonged to a similar figure from the same workshop. The progress towards anatomical accuracy can be followed through the Volomandra kouros (No. 1906) in Room 4, an unequal work of the 550's, and in Room 6 the Anavysos kouros (No. 3851) of the 520's and the kouros of Aristodikos (No. 3938) of about 510. These kouroi are all Attic and, except the one from Sunium, grave monuments. Archaic reliefs are neater and livelier than the statues, since the sculptor had only two dimensions to manage. The gravestone of Aristion (No. 29) in Room 5 is admirable work of its time, about 510, with traces of its original palmette as finial. Back in Room 6 the transition from Archaic to Classical appears in the reliefs from the base for a kouros (No. 3476), on which the ball-players demonstrate the new and twisting poses that were invented just before 500.

The Classical sculpture, mostly reliefs, spreads over a dozen rooms in roughly chronological order. In Room 8 a disc with a female head (No. 3990) of about 460 perhaps represents Selene (the Moon), a minor but exquisite sample of the Early Classical manner. The relief of a young victor crowning himself (No. 3344) is in a robuster style and perhaps ten years earlier. The centre piece of Room 9 is the full-sized bronze statue fished up off Cape Artemisium (No. 15161) and complete except for the eyes. The subject is a javelin-thrower, to judge by the right forefinger, bent back to control the thong that made the javelin rotate in flight, and so the statue represents a victor rather than a god. It was designed for the side view (like a relief) and its musculation, though well observed, is that of a static figure. Its date is the 460's. The so-called Omphalos Apollo (No. 45), a Roman copy of an original of the 450's, is a useful document of the evolution of the Classical male nude from the stiff kouros. A very large relief from Eleusis (No. 126), of about 440, shows a curious juxtaposition of old and new formulas.

The series of Attic grave reliefs, which occupy Rooms 10, 14, 17, 18 and part of 19, is unique. They begin in the later fifth century and continue till about 317, when a law on funeral costs priced them out. The favourite subjects are domestic and even trivial, though not always readily intelligible; the treatment has at first a Classical restraint which later tends to dissolve into emotion; and the quality varies from first to third rate. For a sequence of excellent pieces one might take No. 715 in Room 10 (young man and slave boy, from Salamis) of about 420, No. 3624 (Hegeso's memorial) of the 390's and No. 726 of about 375 (both in Room 14 and representing a seated woman and her slave girl), No. 869 in Room 17 (young man with father and slave boy, from the Ilissus) of the 330's, and No. 833 in Room 19 (standing man and standing woman, from Rhamnus) which is perhaps a little later.

There are other Classical reliefs in Room 11, including fragments from the late fifth century temple at the Argive Heraeum (Nos. 1561–83). Room 12 is a painful tribute to the genius of Phidias, especially when one observes the Varvakeion Athena (No. 129), a vulgar Roman souvenir of the great statue in the Parthenon. Room 15 has more Roman copies. Architectural sculpture from Epidaurus (Nos. 136–62) in Room 16 illustrates the gracefully conservative style of the earlier fourth century, and pedimental fragments from Tegea (Nos. 178–80) in Room 19 a new pathetic trend that begins little if any later. The bronze youth found in the sea off Anticythera (No. 13396 in Room 19), of about 340, shows another development; here the pose is more restless and the figure reaches forward instead of sideways into space.

Not much of the Hellenistic and Roman periods is or deserves to be on view. The heads of the colossal statues of Lycosura (Nos. 1734–7), to be dated in the second century (whether B.C. or A.D.), are in Room 20. Room 21 contains a fragmentary bronze statue of a philosopher (No. 13400) of the third century and dredged up off Cape Artemisium, a marble statue of Posidon from Melos (No. 235) of the second century, a realistic bronze portrait head from Delos (No. 14612), a coyly vulgar marble group of Aphrodite slapping Pan (No. 3335) of the early first century B.C., and some rather later and more chastely decorative 'Neo-Attic' reliefs. There are also grave reliefs of various dates here and in Room 22. Most of these in one way or another show dependence on Classical models. Much more original is the boy jockey (also from the sea off Cape Artemisium), which may be of the third century B.C.: it is, perhaps temporarily, in Room 26.

There is more sculpture in the extension at the back. Room 25 houses a miscellany of mostly indifferent pieces, and two notable bronze statues stand provisionally in Rooms 30 and 31—a kouros of about 520 found in Piraeus and for a change on land, and the youth from the sea off Marathon (No. 15118), a fine and well preserved work of around 340.

BRONZE COLLECTION

The collection of bronze figurines and other objects in Rooms 27 and 28 includes the numerous finds from the Athenian Acropolis and is of primary importance for experts. The art of these figurines began in the eight century B.C. and was at first original and progressive, but when larger sculpture established itself about the middle of the seventh century the figurines generally reflected its style, though the quality of workmanship remained high and poses tended to be freer. Perhaps too many are exhibited to be appreciated with comfort, though most are worth exhibiting.

VASE COLLECTION

The vase collection upstairs (reached from Room 26) begins in earnest with the Early Iron Age. Through perhaps excessive research the great output of Greek pottery with painted decoration has been classified by styles and schools and even painters and so vase painting has become the best understood branch of Greek art. The Protogeometric style evolved from debased Mycenaean in the later eleventh century and is sober and limited, relying on a precise use of abstract ornaments, of which the most characteristic are concentric circles and semi-circles drawn by compasses. Around 900 it was succeeded by the Geometric style, governed by the same principles but less sparing of decoration and especially fond of the hatched meander; from the middle of the eighth century figures of men and animals were admitted, drawn in silhouette according to an appropriately abstract formula. A radical change began about 730 influenced by Syrian models, though the Greek painters adapted rather than copied and soon developed on their own. This Orientalising style is freer and more colourful than Geometric, gives more life and detail to its figures, and accepts free-hand plant ornament. At Corinth, where it began, silhouette was soon re-established for figure-drawing, but now details were engraved (or 'incised'); this is the so-called Black-Figure style which Athens adopted only in the later seventh century. About 530 progressive Attic painters began to turn to the Red-Figure style, in which the figures are outlined on the reddish surface of the pot and their background filled in with the black paint; since the lines of inner detail were drawn and not incised, the Red-Figure style offered a more fluent and expressive medium to artists. This style lasted in Greece till the late fourth century, when vase paint-ing ceased as a serious art. Though at any one time there was usually some general uniformity of style, many Greek cities had their own local school, anyhow till the seventh or sixth century. Of these schools the Athenian (or Attic) was dominant till the third quarter of the eighth century, then the Corinthian till the early sixth century, and after that the Attic school again. A result of this was that very little pottery of other schools, except during its ascendancy the Corinthian, was impor-ted into Attica and, since finds in Attica make up a large part of this collection, its series of Attic pottery is full but other schools are repre-sented scrappily. Further, from the late eighth century on Corinthian and then Attic potters sold much of their painted ware to exporters and, as it happens, the cemeteries of Etruria have been more prolific of first-rate pieces than has Greece, so that those who have seen the Black-Figure and Red-Figure vases of the Louvre or the British Museum may be disappointed in the National Museum. There is one important exception, the Attic White-ground lekythoi, made for funerary offerings from the 460's till about 400 and not much fancied except by Athenians; the drawing was on a white ground with flat washes of colour for the drapery, and at its best the style is effortlessly Classical.

The first gallery on the right has some Bronze Age pottery, a fair show of Attic Protogeometric and a better of Attic Geometric. The Geometric continues in the next gallery, with early Orientalising of the Corinthian and Attic schools (what is called Early Protocorinthian and Early Protoattic). The third gallery has Orientalising from the Cyclades and some clumsy large pots from Eretria, but the showpieces are the exuberant Attic works of the late seventh century (which some call Late Protoattic and others Early Black-Figure). Attic Black-Figure of the sixth century dominates the next two galleries, though there are selections of finds (not only pottery) from the Argive Heraeum, Perachora, Sparta and other sites. The terracotta models of temples in the fourth gallery are interesting as evidence of the unsophisticated style of building around 700. Architecture proper began in Greece about the middle of the seventh century but then developed fast, as is shown on the wall of this gallery by the painted terracotta metopes and antefixes (ornaments for eaves) from a temple built about 630 at Thermon in Aetolia. Though much larger than vase paintings the paintings of these metopes are essentially similar in style, and it was not till the 470's that large-scale painting became more pictorial. Those who are interested in the Etruscan problem may examine the relief from Lemnos in the fifth gallery, since its inscription is in a language related to Etruscan. The sixth gallery offers more Attic Black-Figure and earlier Red-Figure, the seventh Red-Figure and White-ground ware, and the eighth late Red-Figure (not all of it Attic).

JEWELLERY, EPIGRAPHICAL AND NUMISMATIC COLLECTIONS

A fine collection of jewellery is housed in Room 23, on the right of the entrance hall and beyond the Hellenistic sculpture. The Epigraphical Collection opens off Tositsa Street on the south side of the block and is a peaceful building full of the inscribed stones which have contributed so much to our knowledge of the ancient history of Greece and particularly Athens from the fifth century B.C. on. The Numismatic Department, which possesses one of the largest collections of coins minted in Greece, is reached at present from the big doorway further up Tositsa Street. Finally, at the entrance to the Museum, down the right-hand colonnade outside the doors, there is a shop which sells plaster casts of many objects in the Museum and some elsewhere: the prices are reasonable, but the quality is generally inferior.

The Byzantine Museum

The Byzantine Museum, built as a villa for the Duchess of Plaisance, has an atmosphere of leisure. Its exhibits range in date from the fourth to the nineteenth century A.D., but since Athens and Southern Greece were then unimportant the quality is generally provincial. There is a helpful guide book in English. In the entrance hall on the ground floor specimens are set out of the sculpture and architectural decoration of the fourth to the sixth century, not all of them Christian. The next room reproduces the interior of a small basilical church of the type common in Greece in the fifth and sixth centuries, and some pieces of early Christian sculpture are scattered around. The third room contains sculptures of the ninth to the fifteenth century, some showing Frankish or Venetian influence, and a curious set of reliefs even reviving Pagan mythology. The room beyond has been arranged as the interior of a cruciform church of Middle Byzantine style and, since the surviving churches of that period have been stripped or refurnished, this reconstruction is worth memorising. Beyond is another church interior, typical of the time of the Turkish occupation, though the items used come from very different places.

Most of the upper floor is given over to icons, almost all mediocre. The best and oldest, which are Late Byzantine, hang in the second room. There are more icons in the annexe on the east of the courtyard (the 'East Wing'); its south room has a useful arrangement of canonical subjects and the late 'popular' works in its north room are unsophisticated and uncanonical enough to be amusing.

The Benaki Museum

The Benaki Museum was formed by an avid private collector and is displayed in what was his house. The contents include early Medieval textiles from Egypt, velvets and silks from the Mediterranean and the Near East, Chinese pottery, Egyptian antiquities, Islamic pottery, miscellaneous jewellery, icons, vestments, church furniture, and a reconstruction of a Moslem reception room. Of Greek antiquities there are a small assortment in Room BB and some good pieces of jewellery in Room N; two icons (Nos. 1542–3) are attributed to El Greco before he left Crete; but for most visitors the high spots are the relics and especially the pictures of the War of Independence and later events in Greek history (in Rooms Λ, H, Θ and I) and the show of Greek local costumes, not very well set out in nine rooms of the basement.

The Museum of Decorative Art

The Museum of Decorative Arts is in a converted mosque of the eighteenth century opposite the underground station in Monastiraki Square. It is not much visited but has very fine collections of Coptic textiles dating from the second to the seventh century A.D. and of Greek embroideries of the eighteenth and nineteenth centuries. There are also interesting collections of Late Byzantine and more recent Greek pottery, a colourful show of Greek jewellery in the style of the later Turkish period, and inevitably a few more icons.

4 · Attica and Aegina

Ancient Attica (*Fig.* 6), the territory of the city state of Athens, stretched to the divide between Eleusis and Megara, from there north-west to the Cithaeron range, and back eastwards to the sea to include or exclude Oropos. It has a fair number of attractive or interesting sites, though the scenery is usually undistinguished, even where it has not suffered from modern development.

Piraeus

Piraeus is pleasanter in reality than reputation. Though it had three natural harbours and the terrain made it easy to defend, the Athenians preferred to use the open but nearer beach of Phaleron till 493 B.C., when a base was needed for their new navy. So the peninsula was fortified and in the 460's connected with Athens by the Long Walls. By now Piraeus was becoming a prosperous commercial port too and, though it had its ups and downs, remained useful till the fourth century A.D. In the Middle Ages piracy and raiding made coastal towns very vulnerable and even the name of Piraeus was replaced by Porto Leone, after the stone lion or lions then visible among the ruins. It did not revive till Greece became independent.

Inevitably rebuilding has covered or destroyed most of the remains of ancient Piraeus. Along the coast some pieces of the sea wall still stand and less than 200 yards west of the harbour of Zea (Pasalimani) there is a small theatre of the second century B.C., not too well preserved but not Romanised either. The back rows of seats were, unusually for a Greek theatre, not cut into a hillside but supported on radial walls. The Museum, which is next to the theatre, possesses some interesting sculpture. The most remarkable exhibits are the bronze statues of Athena and Artemis of the middle or late fourth century B.C.; they were found near the main harbour in 1959 and were part of a miscellaneous batch of sculpture, presumably waiting for export to Rome. There are also some Classical grave reliefs of fair quality and a series of marble

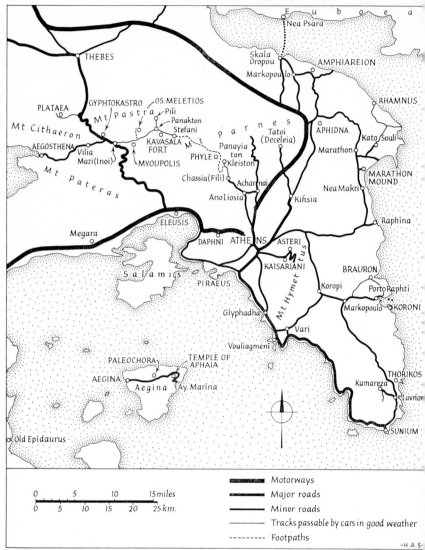

Fig. 6. Attica.

reliefs, dredged up from the sea, which are copies, Roman in date, of the engagements between Greeks and Amazons from the shield of Phidias's great statue of Athena in the Parthenon.

Sunium

Cape Sunium at the south-east corner of Attica is famous for its view and the ruins of its temple of Posidon. It can be reached from Athens either by the highway along the south coast or by the slower road round the north end of Mt Hymettus and through Markopoulo and modern Lavrion. The sanctuary of Posidon was established by the early seventh century B.C., to judge by the offerings discovered, and became important enough to receive several early kouroi, the best preserved of which is the so-called Sunium kouros of the National Museum in Athens. A limestone temple was begun shortly before 480 B.C. but destroyed by the Persians. The present temple is thought to have been built in the late 440's by the architect of the Theseum. Its chief pecularities were the channelling of the columns with sixteen instead of twenty flutes and the carved frieze, which is carried across the front of the cella porch to the outer colonnade. Some badly weathered slabs of this frieze are propped up under a shelter on the left of the path up to the temple. The coarsish marble comes from quarries in the hills two miles to the north and, unlike the marbles of Pentelicon and Hymettus, does not contain iron oxide. So, while the marble buildings of Athens have weathered brown, this temple at Sunium has kept its original dazzling white. There has been some re-erection of columns, which (as old views show) has changed the aspect of this picturesque landmark. How much it was visited by sailors can be judged by the names carved on many of the blocks. Byron too, though he denounced Elgin for carrying off sculpture, was not above vandalism of this sort; at least his name is on one of the eastern columns.

The sanctuary was enclosed, as usual, by a wall and there are traces of a double entrance porch and a stoa. Another wall with towers ran from the sanctuary first north and then westwards to the sea. This fortification goes back to 413 B.C., when the Spartans had set up a permanent camp in Attica, but part of what survives is of Hellenistic date. By its northern end there are cuttings in the rock, probably of the late fourth century B.C., to provide two slips for warships. When considering how the slips were used, one must remember that round the Greek coast sea level has risen by an average of perhaps eight feet since Classical times.

This explains many of the Greek ruins that are now awash or submerged. About a quarter of a mile north-east of the sanctuary of Posidon, on the other side of the road, there was a sanctuary of Athena and a curious temple provided with an outer colonnade only on the east and the south, but nothing much remains to be seen.

Laurium

Laurium used to be the name for all the hilly country which runs north from Sunium. The region was rich in minerals, of which the silver particularly interested the ancients. At what time mining began here is not known, but the lodes were worked very actively from the sixth till the second century B.C. when it was believed that the silver-bearing ores had been exhausted—and indeed, when mining was resumed in 1860, it was now mainly for zinc and manganese. The mines were owned by the state but leased for three to ten years to private citizens, and the labourers were slaves. Though the Athenians prided themselves on treating their slaves humanely, mining was hard and dangerous work and Laurium was conveniently remote. Anyhow conditions cannot have been much different from those made familiar by Hollywood and Cinecittà. The ore was hacked out in galleries up to three feet wide and a few inches higher. Shafts for access and ventilation were usually 80–180 feet deep, though one went down 400 feet. Lighting was by simple oil lamps of terracotta of the household types common in museums. When the ore was brought up from the mine, it was sorted to remove useless rock, crushed manually in mortars or mills and then washed. The washing tables, which vary from 4 to 16 yards across and are coated with cement, consist of a long raised tank, a strip of floor tilting more or less sharply away, and beyond it a larger flatter floor; the first (or washing) floor drains into a channel which runs round the second (or drying) floor, passing through two settling basins, and ends in a third basin near the tank. The crushed ore was spread on the washing floor and water was released from the tank to swill off the lighter constituents. These settled in the basins and, as long as more panning seemed worth it, were scooped up and spread out to dry on the larger floor before being washed again. The water was ladled back from the last basin into the tank, since the miners could not afford to waste it, and similarly the tanks and cisterns (in which the seasonal rainfall was collected) were screened or roofed over to reduce evaporation. After washing the ore was smelted in furnaces and the silver and lead separated by the wasteful method of cupellation. The size of the industry, which made a big contribution to Athenian prosperity, can be judged from ancient records and the remains themselves. There are several valleys where shafts, tunnels, cisterns, washing floors and more rarely ruins of furnaces can be seen all round among the pines and heaps of broken rock. It makes a strangely attractive industrial landscape, which is hardly visited except by the resin-gatherers whose receptacles are fixed to almost every tree. What may be called the upper Agrileza Valley is perhaps the easiest to visit by car. One leaves the modern town of Lavrion at its north end by the poor road east to Kamareza and after 3 miles, at the top of the hill and a little short of Kamareza, turns off to the left along a track. This track keeps to the ridge and after 2 miles comes to a church, and from here it is better to go on foot. Just beyond the church a left fork leads through derelict modern installations and down along the left side of a valley, the slopes and bottom of which are thick with ancient remains, untouched by modern working. Further down a track to the right leads in two hours or less to Sunium, in part following a well preserved ancient causeway, which may have been built to transport marble for the temple of Posidon at Sunium.

Thorikos

Thorikos, a little north of modern Lavrion, was an ancient town and port. It is recognised most easily by its theatre, at the foot of a steep hill to the north of the road to Markopoulo just after it leaves the coast. Access is by a bumpy track. Settlement on the hill had begun by the Middle Bronze Age and later two Mycenanean tholos tombs (badly damaged) were built halfway up its northern and eastern slopes. Further east on the neck of the promontory and overlooking bays on both sides there are the scanty remains of a fortress of the late fifth century B.C. Conveniently the most interesting remains are in the area of the theatre. The theatre itself is abnormal, at least for a permanent structure. Its auditorium makes a flattened irregular curve and the orchestra is roughly oblong, but since its date seems the end of the sixth century B.C. the plan cannot very well be classed as primitive; presumably in the small town of Thorikos economy was more important than convention. A couple of hundred yards west from the theatre there is a ruined ancient tower which was never part of a system of fortification. Towers were common on farms in Attica and elsewhere, but this one is more likely to have served as a strong room, perhaps for silver. Near-by the excavators have found walls of houses, going back to the Classical period, and washing floors for ore. One of these floors is remarkably well preserved.

Brauron

Brauron is a dozen miles north of Thorikos. The sanctuary is now about a quarter of a mile from the sea, but used to be nearer. The usual route to it is by the side road (signposted) a little east of Markopoulo on the road to Porto Raphti. This side road soon gets rough. About a quarter of a mile before the sanctuary a fenced enclosure on the left protects the remains of a large *basilical church* (*Fig.* 7) of the sixth century A.D. and, since it was ruined in the next century, the original plan is not much obscured by alterations. When in the fourth century Christianity became the official religion of the Roman Empire and there was a spate of church building, the model generally approved was that of the civil basilica, a type of large hall used for law courts, markets and other gatherings. Ideally the basilica consisted of a broad, high nave that

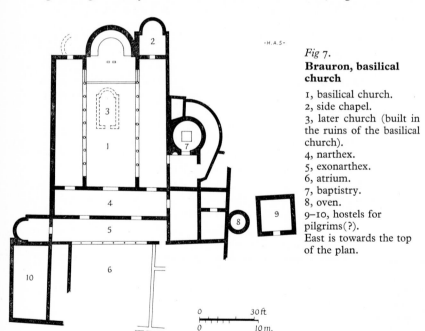

-H.A.S-

Fig 7.
Brauron, basilical church

1, basilical church.
2, side chapel.
3, later church (built in the ruins of the basilical church).
4, narthex.
5, exonarthex.
6, atrium.
7, baptistry.
8, oven.
9–10, hostels for pilgrims(?).
East is towards the top of the plan.

0   30 ft
0   10 m.

ended in an apse and, separated from it by columns or piers, two narrower and lower aisles; the nave had a low-pitched gabled roof and clerestory windows, and the aisles had penthouse roofs. The two churches of St Apollinaris at Ravenna are examples of the type, as is the rebuilt church of St Demetrius at Thessalonica. The early basilical churches show regional differences and they developed differently: in the Latin West the church with aisle and naves is still standard, but in the Orthodox East the centralised church began to replace the basilica in the fifth and sixth centuries A.D.

The basilica at Brauron is fairly typical of the version current in Greece—a church with narthex (that is a closed vestibule across the front end) and in front of the narthex a squarish courtyard (or 'atrium'). The apsidal chapel projecting from the south aisle is an unfortunate excrescence and the curving wall attached to the north aisle a later and clumsy addition. The internal arrangements reflect the hierarchical organisation which official Christianity copied from the State. The bishop had his throne in the apse behind the altar and the presbyters sat on the bench round the wall. Lesser clergy took their places at the sides of the nave within the altar rails. The rest of the nave remained clear for processions and ceremonials, the aisles contained the qualified laity, and penitents and persons under instruction were restricted to the narthex. The foundations placed eccentrically in the middle of the nave are of a little church built after the basilica was in ruins. The exonarthex, in front of the narthex, acts as a colonnaded side of the atrium. The round structure which adjoins the south aisle was a baptistery. Other buildings served the resident clergy and perhaps pilgrims.

A little white chapel marks the site of the Pagan *sanctuary of Brauronian Artemis* which goes back (it seems) to the late eighth century, had its heyday in the fifth and fourth centuries, and was then ruined by flooding. This sanctuary is famous for the 'Bears', Athenian girls of good family, who were brought here in childhood and stayed on as attendants till they married. The ancients understood the custom no better than we do and the explanation they gave was that it was an expiation for the killing of a she-bear which was under the protection of Artemis. The Brauronion on the Athenian Acropolis was affiliated to this sanctuary. On the rise beside the chapel the plan of the temple, Doric of the fifth century, can be made out, and below it on the west was the holy spring. To the north a large court was constructed around 425 B.C. It is open to the south, where it meets the rock, and at the opposite end had a Doric colonnade (now partly restored) with one column returning on each side;

the reconstruction includes the frieze and gives an example of the management of triglyphs at an inner corner. Behind on the west and north were the dormitories of the Bears, each provided with eleven beds and stone tables—the slots and fastenings for the bed legs remain. Behind the northern dormitories there was a wide corridor, entered at each end by imposing doors, as cuttings in the thresholds show. Statues of 'Bears' and votive reliefs stood in this corridor and in the colonnade against the dormitory walls. To the west of the court and on a different alignment is a very solid low bridge with cart ruts crossing it obliquely; presumably these ruts were made when the sanctuary had decayed and become marsh. South-east of the temple there is a cleft through the hillside with the remains of unpretentious buildings and a collapsed cave, which was already a place of some holiness in the eighth century. The flooding of the sanctuary in the late fourth century B.C. preserved a remarkable assortment of finds. Besides the inevitable pottery there are statues of the child she-bears (more sentimental than might be expected of Classical sculptors), several excellent reliefs, and thousands of small objects, some of them of wood. All these are now in the Museum to the south-east of the sanctuary. Brauron is a site of unusual charm.

On the hill above the sanctuary the Greek excavators report finds that show settlement from the Late Neolithic to the Late Bronze Age, but afterwards it seems that the site was deserted.

From the sanctuary a track no rougher than that from Markopoulo leads in 4 miles to *Porto Raphti*. One starts towards the south-east below the chapel, after a few hundred yards bears left, and then continues forward up and down hill. Porto Raphti is a pleasant sea-side village with simple restaurants. It gets its name—Port Tailor—from a traditional misinterpretation of the battered colossal statue of a seated woman set up in Roman times on the top of the island at the mouth of the bay. Across the bay on the peninsula of *Koroni* there is in the scrub a fortified camp which looks very early, but was constructed by Ptolemy II of Egypt in the 260's B.C. Keen students of military history might find a visit interesting.

Marathon

The plain of Marathon is famous for the battle of 490 B.C., where a Persian punitive force was beaten unexpectedly by the Athenians and the Plataeans. (The Plataeans do not usually get the credit they deserve, since the Persians had nothing against them and they were only honouring an alliance with Athens.) The mound under which the Athenian dead were buried is down a side road on the right, clearly signposted, just beyond Nea Makri on the road to the present village of Marathon. At the foot of the mound is a bowdlerised modern version of the earlier grave-stone of Aristion, which was found some miles to the south. From the top the historically or romantically gifted can refight the battle. The Marathon plain is fertile and had its wealthy lords in the Bronze Age, to judge by legend and a recently discovered tholos tomb of the fourteenth century B.C. It lies a little more than a mile west of the mound, but with-out local advice is not easy to find among the market gardens. Unusually the tholos is sunk in the level ground, although the hill begins only a few hundred yards away. The cap, which projects a few feet above ground is restored. Near the beginning of the entrance passage two horses were buried; their bones used to be under the rusty iron box in the floor. Though not one of the more elaborate tholos tombs, it has a grim attractiveness. Up the valley 55° W from the mound and about 3 miles distant was, much later, the country home of the ubiquitous Herodes Atticus. Another $1\frac{1}{2}$ miles beyond is one of the many ancient caves of Pan.

Rhamnus

Rhamnus is about 10 miles by road beyond the mound of Marathon. At the north end of the plain one takes the side road to the right for Kato Souli, there turns left along a rough track, after 3 miles forks left, and in another 3 miles arrives at the gate of the fenced and desolate archaeological zone. The sanctuary, just inside the gate, has two ruined temples, huddled awkwardly and obliquely together, and a terrace. Both were dedicated to Nemesis and Themis. The smaller temple, whether late Archaic or archaising, was built of fine polygonal masonry and did not have an outer colonnade. The other temple had a colonnade and is thought to have been built in the 430's by the architect of the Theseum. The details of Greek temples were often unfinished, but not often as unfinished as here. Not only were steps and floor slabs left with their protective surfaces, but the columns remained unfluted. Still the main structure was complete enough to house Agoracritus's colossal statue of Nemesis, a piece of whose head was found by Gandy and given to the British Museum. Round the sanctuary are broken ancient gravestones. A path leads down to the shore, where the ancient fortress of Rhamnus stood on a small hill between two sandy beaches. There are substantial

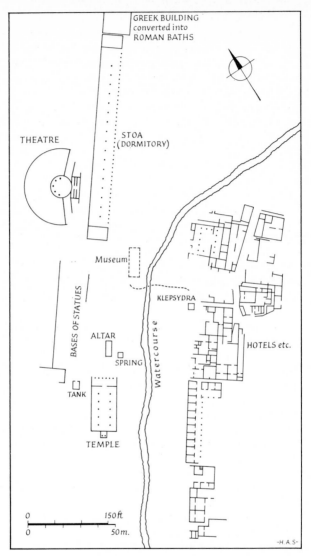

Fig. 8. The Amphiareion (Oropos).

remains of the outer wall with towers and gate, and within it, over-grown by scrub, traces of houses, a theatre and a citadel. The citadel should be no later than the fifth century, the outer fortifications (which were added afterwards) probably of around 400 B.C. Traces of more houses appear outside the wall on the south-east. Set against the background of the sea and Euboea, this fortress is one of the picturesque sites of Attica.

The Amphiareion   (*Fig.* 8)

The Amphiareion of Oropos is a prettier spot. The most direct route from Athens is to follow the National Road for about 20 miles and then turn off right along a signposted side road, which leads in 10 miles to the sanctuary; or one can continue on the road through Marathon and join the same side road. Skala Oropou, with its car-ferry to Nea Psara (the ancient Eretria) in Euboea, is 5 miles beyond the sanctuary, turning right at another Markopoulo. The district of Oropos belonged originally to Boeotia but was annexed to Attica in 506–411, 386–366, 338–322, 156–86, and finally from the last quarter of the first century B.C. The patron of the sanctuary, Amphiaraus, was a legendary king of Argos with a gift for prophecy, whose wife sent him to his death at Thebes in return for the necklace of Harmonia. Heroes were semi-divine, and Amphiaraus's spirit remained prophetic, specialising—anyhow by the end of the fifth century—in medical advice. As at many Greek sanctuaries the legends do not give a satisfactory explanation of the origins of the cult, which presumably had been forgotten.

The site, excavated by the Greeks, is entered at the south-west and the first ruin is the temple. This curious building has a broad cella with two inner rows of columns, no outer colonnade, six columns between antae at its east (more strictly north-east) end, and in the middle of the west end a protruding little porch of two columns. Estimates of the date range from the fifth to the third century B.C.; the latest seems to us the most credible. The arm of a colossal marble statue has been left lying in the cella. In front of the temple stands the altar, and between it and the gully the sacred spring still flows. Further on a long stoa, built in the early fourth century B.C., served as a dormitory for patients, probably males in the main hall and women in the two small end rooms; some of the benches they slept on have survived. The routine was for the patient to drink no wine for three days, fast for one, and then sleep in the stoa to be given a prescription in a dream; the priests helped to interpret and, anyhow from Hellenistic times, there was professional medical advice as well. In front of the stoa an excellent gutter carried off rainwater, and to avoid damp space was left between the rear wall of the stoa and the retaining wall behind. The little theatre at the back of the stoa was used for the musical events of the four-yearly games which were instituted in 332 B.C. Its stage front, now re-erected, is thought to have been built about 200 B.C., when stone stages were coming into fashion; but the upper storey, which served as a back-cloth and has not been restored, is put fifty years later. The side entrances and the five seats of honour are attributed to the early first century B.C. Beyond the stoa a building of unknown purpose was replaced by baths in the Roman period, and on the other side of the gully there are stumps of walls of large houses and hotels, difficult to make out even with a plan, and also a remarkably well preserved water-clock (or 'klepsydra'). This installation, which is a little to the right of the crossing of the gully (between the Museum and the temple), has its tank and outlet pipe intact; the float by which the passage of time was indicated has of course perished. The small Museum and its courtyard exhibit a reconstruction of the entablature of the temple, various architectural fragments, inscriptions, and pieces of sculpture (nearly all Roman).

Attic Fortresses

The northern frontier of Attica, running along Mts Parnes and Cithaeron, was unusually well defended by fortresses, which were also places of refuge for the inhabitants of the outlying districts. Rhamnus on the east coast protected the sea crossing to Euboea, but the others overlooked the principal land routes from Boeotia. Their garrisons could not have been big enough to stop an invading army, but when such an army had passed they could interrupt its supplies and they deterred small parties of raiders. Aphidna and Deceleia (Tatoi) guarded the roads to Oropos and Tanagra, Phyle and Kavasala (perhaps the ancient Panakton) one road to Thebes and Myoupolis (probably Oinoe) and Gyphtokastro (perhaps Eleutherae) the other. The dates of these fortresses are uncertain and even their identification, since the references in ancient literature are insufficient, inscriptions are lacking (except at Rhamnus), the style of masonry can be only a rough guide, and if there has been excavation it has not usually produced helpful contexts. In general fortified posts had been established by the end of the fifth century B.C., but though parts of the early walls survive the more con-

spicuous defences are of the fourth or third centuries. Very little remains
of Aphidna and Deceleia, but *Phyle* is impressive. It is reached from
Athens by the road from Ano Liosia to Chassia (now officially Fili)
Some motoring maps show this road continuing past ancient Phyle and
over the mountains to Boeotia, but as a road it stops below the monastery
of Panayia ton Kleiston. From there it is about an hour and a quarter on
foot to the fortress which stands on a hill to the north-west. *Kavasala*,
five hours walk north-west of Phyle, is approached more easily by a
rough track (passable by cars) that runs east from Mazi, which is about
30 miles from Athens on the main road past Eleusis to Thebes. This
track serves for Myoupolis as well as Kavasala. *Myoupolis* is on the right
after 2 miles; it was a rectangular fortress on fairly level ground. Just
beyond the track divides. The left fork leads in 2 miles to the important
monastery of *Osios Meletios*, with a church that goes back to about 1100.
The other fork after 5 miles passes below Kavasala, which is on the hill
on the right but not easily seen from below. *Gyphtokastro* is more convenient to visit and better preserved. It stands conspicuously on a hill
to the right of the road to Thebes as it begins to climb the pass above
Mazi and the easiest entrance is round the corner from the north-west.
The outer wall, which was built perhaps in the early fourth century
B.C., is in excellent condition on the north side. The walk along its top
passes through the small towers to allow the defenders mobility and
there are gates or posterns on all sides. Even when designing for utility,
Classical and Hellenistic masons liked to keep their courses precisely
regular and often contrived a little elegance in the drafting of corners.
Inside near the middle of the north wall the ruins of a sort of keep of
rougher construction look like an earlier fortlet. Below Gyphtokastro
to the east of the road there are the foundations of two early basilical
churches, and near Mazi on the roadside a ruined ancient tower of not
very obvious purpose.

Aegosthena   (*Fig.* 9)

Just below Gyphtokastro a side road leads westward through Vilia and
after 13 miles ends at Aegosthena (or Porto Yermeno) between Mts
Cithaeron and Pateras at the head of the Halcyonian Gulf. Here on a
rise in the valley there was a small fortified town. The frontier between
the territories of Athens and Megara followed the hills a little west of
the modern road from Eleusis to Thebes, and so Aegosthena was
Megarian. Its strategic importance was that it lay on a route which,

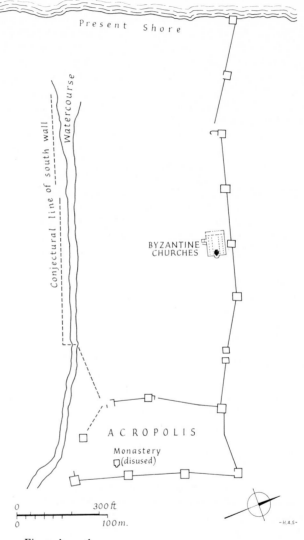

Fig. 9. Aegosthena.

though neglected now, led directly from Megara to Boeotia and also by-passed an often hostile Attica, nor indeed was access to Attica always so convenient; at least finds show that in the early fourth century B.C. the red-figure pottery used in Aegosthena was made in Corinth and not the generally preferred Athenian product. It is easy to overlook the changes in direction of approach which have been made by modern motor roads.

The fortified area of Aegosthena is nearly 600 yards long by 200 wide, with an acropolis at the east or inland end and the lower town running down to the sea. It is not certain whether there was a wall along the shore; the south wall, which ran beside the stream bed, has almost completely disappeared; but the north wall still stands to a fair height and has an interesting gateway about 140 yards from the sea. The acropolis is more impressive for both situation and preservation. The inner western fortification has been replaced by a poorly built retaining wall, but the eastern stretch of towers and curtains gives an excellent idea of its original state and the corner tower at the south-east (about 46 feet high) is as fine as any Greek tower that survives and has lost only its wooden floor and roof. These fortifications are much higher than those of Gyphtokastro and the corner towers were strengthened in their lower parts to resist battering rams or catapults. Those at the north-west and north-east of the acropolis are filled with 10 feet of rubble, the one at the south-east (which is threatened from higher ground outside) has nearly 20 feet of filling—almost to the level of the door on its inner face. There are good views of the eastern wall from outside this tower and also from the road as it winds down towards the fortress, but for photographers the light is better in the morning. Aegosthena is mentioned very rarely by ancient writers and for the date of the fortifications we have to guess by historical probabilities and the style of the masonry, which differs in the towers and the walls, though the reason for this difference is more likely to be structural or aesthetic than chronological. Still, it is safe to say that both walls and towers are of the fourth or third century B.C., though the site was inhabited much earlier.

Inside the fortress the visible remains are Christian. A small church and the ruins of a small monastery stand on the acropolis. A couple of hundred yards lower down near the north wall there is another and better church, externally cruciform though the side arms are no more than apses inside. It too belonged to a monastery, which was occupied in the eleventh and twelfth centuries. This church was built inside the ruins of a much larger basilical church, probably of the sixth century,

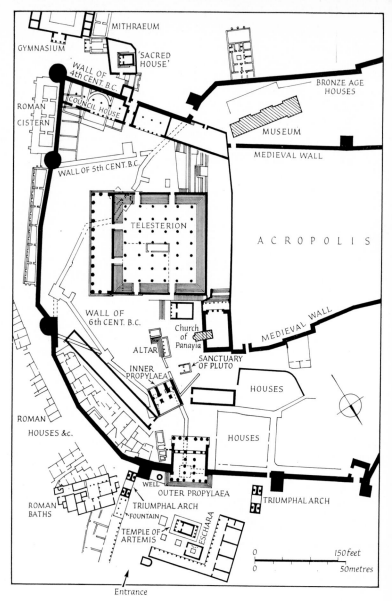

Fig. 10. Eleusis, Sanctuary of Demeter.

and is placed precisely within the east end of the nave of its predecessor. Excavation has shown that the basilica, which measured about 84 by 68 feet, had a nave ending in an apse, two pairs of aisles, a narthex, and —opening off the south side—a rectangular baptistery. Patches of the original mosaic floor of the nave and narthex survive. The ruins are complicated by the later monastic buildings, though they made more use than might be expected of the abandoned basilica.

Eleusis   (*Fig.* 10)

Eleusis is just off the main road, 13 miles west of Athens. Here a low hill runs beside the shore of a sheltered bay and a fertile plain stretches some five miles inland with natural barriers to west and east. Occupation of the hill had begun by the Early Bronze Age and it was closely settled from soon after 2000 B.C. till Byzantine times. At first, according to legend and common sense, Eleusis was an independent state, but at some unknown date it was annexed to Attica, though with a privileged status. Its reputation was made by the sanctuary of Demeter, which was developed in the sixth century B.C. and prospered increasingly into Roman times, so much so that when Sarmatian raiders broke through in A.D. 170 the damage was repaired at once by the Emperor Marcus Aurelius and it was not until the last years of the fourth century that the invasion of Alaric and Christian antagonism put an end to both cult and sanctuary. Demeter was the goddess of corn, revered throughout Greece, but Eleusis somehow acquired primacy and the Eleusinian Mysteries became the most famous in Greece. Though the number of initiates was very large, they were vowed to secrecy and this prevented at least any written record of the principal ceremony, but from the respectability of some later adherents it cannot have been grossly orgiastic. The attraction of the Mysteries was that while still acknowledging the established Pagan religion they promised initiates, without distinction of status or sex or nationality, some sort of existence after death. Even Roman Emperors accepted initiation.

The highest part of the hill of Eleusis became of course its acropolis, the town stretched westwards, the sanctuary was built on and into the eastern slope, and as prosperity increased a sort of suburb grew up around. The ancient acropolis and town have suffered badly from medieval houses and defences, and the principal excavation (carried on by the Greeks) has been in the area of the sanctuary. Though—through no fault of the excavators—the site is messy and its environment unsavoury, Eleusis is hallowed ground for social anthropologists, if they are interested in ancient Greece.

The modern entrance to the sanctuary opens onto a paved court in front of the ancient Outer Propylaea. Here the surviving remains are mostly of the Roman period. On the right there were a temple of Artemis and altars. Further right and near the fortification wall a 'triumphal arch' has been traced by the excavators. Opposite, on the left side of the court, a corresponding arch can be made out; it leads to the ruins of Roman baths and hotels or houses. In the corner on the left of the Propylaea a fairly preserved well goes back perhaps to the sixth century B.C. The Propylaea itself, which replaced an earlier defensive gate, is a scale copy of the central block of the Propylaea of the Athenian Acropolis but adjusted for level ground. Parts of the superstructure are spread out in front, including the central feature of one of its pediments, the bust of a Roman Emperor protruding from a frame like an advertisement for Players' cigarettes. If, as is likely, this is Marcus Aurelius, the Outer Propylaea should have been built in the A.D. 170's. Passing through, one has on the right the ruins of Roman and earlier houses, which were outside the sanctuary, and half-left the smaller Inner Propylaea, built for the Roman consul Appius Claudius Pulcher soon after the middle of the first century B.C. This too is on the site of a former gate. On its inner face the entablature was supported by two Caryatids, of which the better preserved is in the Museum on the hill and the other (now in Cambridge, England) was buried to the neck in manure by the Eleusinians of the early nineteenth century, so promoting the fertility of their crops. Since during and after the Middle Ages piracy depopulated so many island and coastal villages and Eleusis (like much of Attica, Boeotia and the Argolid) was resettled with Albanians, this ritual may be not a garbled survival of the old cult of Demeter, but a medieval or modern invention inspired by the ears of corn carved on the cylinders which rest on the Caryatids' heads. To the right of the Inner Propylaea is the precinct and cave of Pluto (or Hades), connecting with the underworld, and ahead the road with its Roman paving leads up to the Telesterion.

The Telesterion, where the secret ceremony of the Mysteries took place, was necessarily a closed hall and its final extent can be judged from the steps which ran round its walls on the inside and should be completed to form a square. In the north-eastern half of this building one can see and perhaps distinguish by position and style of masonry some remains of its predecessors, which were buried and preserved as the terrace of the Telesterion was extended. The earliest structure on this site was a simple Mycenaean building, which was set on a slightly different alignment, and a curved stretch of wall crossing this at the south is probably of the eighth century B.C. Whether these buildings were or were not religious cannot be proved, but an oblong building of the late seventh century, which cuts across the Mycenaean walls, was pretty certainly a Telesterion. In the second half of the sixth century this was superseded and its remains enclosed by a square building with a portico of nine columns in front and five rows of five columns inside to support the roof. After the Persian destruction of 480–79 B.C. the north-east and south-west walls of this Pisistratean Telesterion were re-used for an oblong building with three rows of internal columns and planned to stretch further up and down the slope. This project, it seems, was not completed and instead the present Telesterion, rather more than twice as large and again square, was erected about the middle of the fifth century. It had steps against the walls to give the congregation a better view, seven rows of six two-tiered columns to carry the roof (though foundations show that the original plan was for five rows of four single columns) and probably a small clerestory in the middle. In the later fourth century B.C. a porch, never finished in detail, was attached by Philo to the south-east side. This was the final form, and the operations after the damage of A.D. 170 were no more than slovenly repairs. As the earliest known example of a large closed hall built by Greeks, the Periclean Telesterion is prominent in handbooks on Classical architecture. Ictinus, one of the two architects of the Parthenon, had a share in this design too.

The steps beyond the Telesterion may well be Roman. To the south in the corner of the fortification a Council House was built in the third century B.C. and replaced by a stoa and other structures in Roman times. Below and to the east of the Telesterion are walls of store rooms, mostly Roman. If there was a temple of Demeter, separate from the Telesterion, it has not been identified convincingly.

The wall enclosing the sanctuary was also part of the defences of Eleusis. The earliest fortification that has been discovered is of the later sixth century B.C. It encircled the hill and in the sanctuary area made a right angle turn under the Outer Propylaea, bent out to provide a gate under the Inner Propylaea, continued south to just below the east corner of the Telesterion, and turned west to run under its south corner and on past the Museum. It was built of mud brick on a stone base and some of these bricks can be seen under a modern shelter near the east

corner of the Telesterion. Soon after 480 B.C. an extension was built on
the east, running in a curve from the Outer Propylaea (where a gate was
made) to the corner of the sixth-century wall; and a few years later this
extension had to be continued just past the enlarged Telesterion, returning along its further side. In the fourth century a further acute-
angled extension was added at the south. Good specimens of the
masonry of the two last periods can be seen at the south-east, anyhow in
the lower courses, since (as often happens where a wall continued in use)
there was later rebuilding of the upper parts. The earlier fortifications
that became unnecessary because of extensions were usually demolished,
unless wanted to retain terraces.

For most visitors it is a relief to come to the Museum, up the steps
beyond the Telesterion. It has a fair assortment of sculpture; the useful
series of pottery includes an Attic amphora of about 660 B.C., nearly
5 feet high and decorated clumsily even for its time with paintings of the
blinding of Polyphemus and the death of Medusa; and a long piece of
linen is the only specimen of that material which has survived from
Classical Greece. The persevering can continue past the Museum along
the south slope of the hill, where a jumble of low walls represents houses
of the Middle Bronze, Mycenaean and Early Iron Ages, as well as of
later times.

Aegina

The island of Aegina rises from the middle of the Saronic Gulf, about
12 miles from the coast of Attica of which it is now officially a part. It is
triangular in shape, measuring about 8 miles along each side. The
ancient and modern town is round the north-west corner, the temple of
Aphaia at the north-east, and the familiar landmark of the conical
mountain at the south end. Ships sail regularly between Piraeus and the
town, from which buses and taxis run to near the temple, so that one can
return to Athens the same day; and in summer one-day cruises from
Piraeus to Hydra (Idhra) and back call at Ayia Marina for a short visit
to the temple.

Aegina has been inhabited since the Neolithic period, with inter-
missions caused by piracy or war. Its greatest prosperity was in the
Archaic period, when also it was a partner in the Greek commercial
concession at Naucratis in Egypt and produced noted sculptors. About
456 B.C. it surrendered to Athens, was afterwards always dependent on
one or other of the dominant powers, and by Roman times had sunk into

poverty and been robbed of most of its works of art. In the Middle Ages it suffered under the Byzantines, Franks, Catalans, and Venetians, and in 1537 was taken by the Turks, who held it—except for a Venetian reoccupation from 1687–1715—till the War of Independence. Then it had a patch of glory, as capital of free Greece from 1826 till 1828.

The ancient city stretched north beyond the modern town round a little headland. This was the nucleus of the original settlement, but the robbing of stone down to the last century has left little more to see than a single column of a late Archaic temple, probably of Apollo, and traces of a theatre. The Museum does not offer much except to those interested in pottery. About a mile along the road to the temple of Aphaia a path on the left leads to a little church called Omorphi Ekklesia, consisting of a single barrel-vaulted nave; it was built of ancient material near the end of the thirteenth century and the paintings on its walls are not much later. About 5 miles from the modern town, also on the left of the road, the deserted site of Palaeochora can be seen on the hillside. This replaced the town by the harbour about A.D. 900, when the Aeginetans had to find a place safer from or for piracy, and was not abandoned till the early nineteenth century. It has more than twenty decaying or restored churches, mostly of the thirteenth and fourteenth centuries and modest in quality; some still have paintings on their walls in various styles of the Venetian and Turkish periods. There are also ruins of houses and monasteries, though much of the stone has been taken away for re-use, and at the top stands a Venetian fortress.

The temple of Aphaia is at the top of a hill, happily set against pine trees. It was the third temple on the site and must have been built around 490 B.C. The outer colonnade is very well preserved, the inner (which has two tiers) is restored. In the columns at the east, as often in Greek temples, there are cuttings for a metal grille. The material used for the building is a local limestone, originally coated with stucco, according to the normal practice of good Greek architecture; buildings of marble were in general rare and their frequency in Attica is explained by the exceptional wealth of Classical Athens and the proximity of marble quarries. For sculpture, though, the Greeks did not think limestone a satisfactory material, and the figures which decorated the pediments of Aphaia were of imported marble. Most of them were found in 1811 and bought for Munich, but some later finds are in the National Museum in Athens. The subjects of both pediments are soldiers fighting and Athena by herself in the centre, but for the space available there are too many figures in the style of each pediment—why, is still a puzzle.

The altar contemporary with the existing temple stood at the foot of the access ramp; the entrance to the sanctuary, which of course was walled, opened at the south-east, so giving an oblique view of the temple; and further east there were rooms presumably used for festivals.

The mountain at the south of the island (which like most of the mountains of small Greek islands is called St Elias) provides as good a view as one would expect. At the top there was once an altar of Zeus Hellanios and at the north foot his sanctuary. Of the sanctuary there remain—from a reconstruction in the second century B.C.—part of the massive terrace wall, a stairway and some relics of a large hall.

5 · Corinth and its Neighbourhood

Old Corinth is at the north-east corner of the Peloponnese (*Fig.* 11), near the Isthmus. From Athens a fast road passes Eleusis and Megara (with its shabby remains of an ancient fountain) and on the outskirts of modern Corinth branches west for Patras and south for the Argolid. From both these main roads there are turnings off for Old Corinth (Palaia Korinthos) though the view of Acrocorinth is better from the Argos route. The distance from Athens is about 56 miles. Modern Corinth has hotels, but for the visitor with a car there is more comfort at Loutraki, round the bay across the canal.

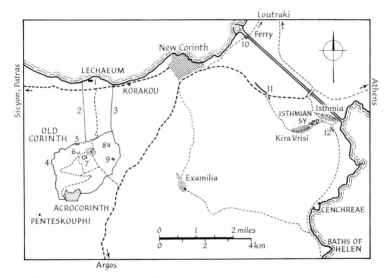

Fig. 11. **Corinth and the Isthmus**
1, basilical church. 2–3, line of Long Walls. 4, line of city wall. 5, Lerna and Asklepieion. 6, theatre. 7, Agora. 8, amphitheatre. 9, basilical church. 10, diolkos. 11, Justinian's wall. 12, Mycenaean wall. Roads are shown by broken lines.

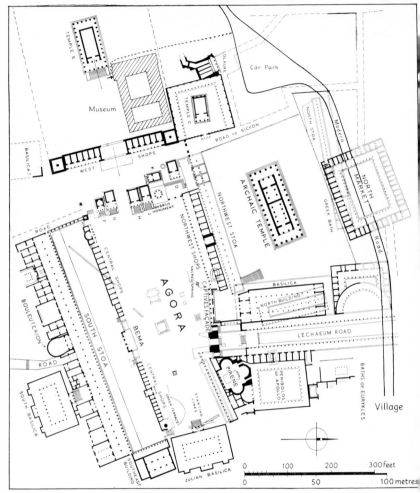

Fig. 12. Corinth, central area.
By courtesy of the American School of Classical Studies at Athens

Old Corinth

(*Figs.* 11 and 12, *Plate* 7)

The Isthmus, not quite four miles wide, is the only land connection between continental Greece and the Peloponnese and narrow enough to carry cargoes across, since for sailing ships the voyage round the Peloponnese was dangerous as well as long. So in times of commercial

Plate 7.
Air view of
Corinth from the
north-north-west.

or military activity this neck of land was very important. As it happens, there was no good site on or near the Isthmus for a Greek acropolis of normal size and even ancient Corinth, which came to control it, was not properly defensible until its fortifications included the high mass of Acrocorinth, itself more suitable as a place of refuge than of habitation. Indeed the full circuit of these fortifications, the line of which was dictated more or less by the terrain, was more than 6 miles, and that without the two long walls connecting the city with its nearer port. So Corinth needed a largish population before it could take full advantage of its position.

Old Corinth is one of several places in the neighbourhood where remains have been found of Neolithic, Early Bronze Age and Middle Bronze Age villages. From the Mycenaean period there is remarkably little, but of course relatively little of the site has been excavated. Certainly there was occupation in the Early Iron Age and during the eighth century B.C. Corinth was growing prosperous. From some remains a mile to the west an extensive city wall of the seventh century has been claimed and denied; for about a hundred and fifty years till the early sixth century Corinth was the most progressive centre of Greek art and in touch with the East; and it became and remained the principal place for trade with the West, that is Italy and Sicily. Though the city was inland, nearly 2 miles from the western and about 6 from the eastern sea, it had ports on each—Lechaeum and Cenchreae—and there was a Corinthian navy. Its territory now reached to the watershed on the south and south-east (except where Cleonae owned its little inland plain) and to the Sicyonian boundary 5 miles away on the west, and across the Isthmus it took in the promontory of Perachora and the coast to the east as far as the Scironian rocks, which before the modern railway and roads were engineered made the land passage to Megara difficult. During the fifth century B.C. Corinth was threatened commercially by the growing strength of Athens, but survived and prospered more. In 338 Philip of Macedon chose Corinth as the meeting place for his conference of Greek states, for two centuries the possession of Acrocorinth was a principal aim of rival powers, and in 146 after the mishandling of their envoys the Romans destroyed the impudent city and carried off or sold its portable works of art. It was refounded by Julius Caesar in 44 B.C. with colonists recruited from Italians and freed slaves, though Greek soon became its ordinary language again, and in 27 B.C. was promoted to be capital of the province of Achaea, as the Romans named southern Greece. Roman Corinth was a successful city, in contrast to the general economic decay of most of Greece and in spite of the earthquakes to which the district is liable. Then it was ravaged by the Herulians in A.D. 267, by Alaric in 395, by earthquake in 551, by the Slavs in the next two centuries and, when after the tenth century it was reviving, by a Norman raid in 1147. After this the main settlement was on Acrocorinth, usually garrisoned by aliens. Under the Turks a small town grew up a little north of the old city centre, but when this was wrecked by the earthquake of 1858 most of the inhabitants took themselves and the name of Corinth to the new site on the coast 4 miles away. Old Corinth remains as a small village and an archaeological site.

The eminence crowned by the seven columns of the temple of Apollo has been for a long time the most conspicuous feature of ancient Corinth. Originally it was more of a headland than a hill, but in the Archaic and Classical periods the neck of the ridge was quarried away to a depth that can be gauged by the surviving cube of natural rock which contains the fountain of Glauke. Stray finds and graves show that from the beginning this area was inhabited, reasonably enough since there is a good supply of water at Pirene. When at last the city developed and public spaces and buildings became necessary, private housing was pushed further back—a process that continued at least from Archaic to Hellenistic times. Unfortunately we know very little of Greek (and even less of earlier) Corinth. After the Roman destruction of the city in 146 B.C. the site was deserted for a century, and apart from the temple of Apollo, the South Stoa and the North-West Stoa the ruins found by the new colonists were useful only as a source of building stone. Further, Roman Corinth prospered and its substantial remains cover, where they did not uproot, many of the traces of their precursors.

The Temple of Apollo is the earliest surviving structure of importance and from its hill there is a good prospect of the site. If one is not concerned too much with time and motion, this is the place to start the tour. The temple was built about 540 B.C. and after the Heraeum at Olympia is the oldest in Greece which now has columns standing. Early features are the high ratio of length to breadth (fifteen by six columns), the squatness of these columns, and the spread of their capitals; but here —in contrast to the Heraeum—the Doric style of architecture, which was probably created or evolved at Corinth, appears self-assured and was already experimenting with refinements. The material is the local limestone, coated with stucco, of which there are still patches on some of the fallen shafts; the thin coat is Greek, the thick coat that in places overlies it a Roman renewal. This temple had a hip-roofed predecessor of the middle of the seventh century, with terracotta roof tiles of a complexity which argues that tiled roofs were then a new invention. Similar tiles have turned up at the Isthmian Sanctuary and Perachora.

Other Archaic structures which have been found are the Sacred Spring and probably the little apsidal temple below the hill on the south, the fountain of Glauke (which can hardly have been fed by a natural spring) and the fountain of Pirene. The slope on which the city grew has, below what top soil there may be, a bed of conglomerate, generally 5 to 6 feet thick and resting on white clay. In some places there was limestone above the conglomerate, as round Temple Hill, but since this is good building stone much of it was quarried away. The rain soaks through the conglomerate and drains along the surface of the clay to come out in springs at the edge of the slope. At Pirene the flow was increased by tunnelling back at the top of the clay, and indeed its discovery by the Americans (who excavate Corinth) was made by crawling along a tunnel. In all there are nearly two miles of tunnels behind Pirene, some of them as old as the Archaic period. In the fifth century, and probably well before then, an irregular Agora had been marked off, running up roughly to the line of the Central Shops; the surface was not yet levelled. Building carried out during this and the next century included the Triglyph Wall near the Sacred Spring, a small temple and the market in the Pirene valley, a stoa and baths on the north side of the hill, the Theatre, and the South Stoa (which bounded a much enlarged Agora). In the next centuries the North-West Stoa was added and there were general improvements. This list, of course, gives only those major works from the Greek period of which traces can be seen. The other ruins are mostly Roman.

A staircase contemporary with the temple leads down from the hill at its south-east corner. In this area the high ruins are the North-West Shops, built in the third century A.D.; the central vault, later converted into a church, was masked externally by a pediment. Behind the Shops was the Greek North-West Stoa, of the third century B.C., and in their eastern range but at a lower level there are the foundations of the apsidal temple, probably of the sixth century B.C. Just south of this temple are the Triglyph Wall and the Sacred Spring. The Triglyph Wall, constructed around 450 B.C., had one metope that pivoted and gave access to an underground passage which runs under the temple and seems to have communicated with it by a small hole in the floor; presumably we have here the mechanism for some pious fraud. The Sacred Spring was roofed over at the time the Triglyph Wall was built: inside, if the guard will unlock the grille, one can see two bronze spouts in the shape of lions' heads, good work of the early fifth century B.C.

The Greek Agora kept the natural slope more or less and its surface was never better than cobbles, patches of which still survive near the east end. Besides being the commercial and political centre it served also as a stadium, and two sets of stone starting lines with grooves close together for the runners' feet can be seen at the east end. As is evident the track was realigned, probably in the Hellenistic period. The Romans characteristically levelled the Agora and paved it with marble, but because of the gradient found it more convenient to make two terraces, the upper retained by the Central Shops, built in the first century A.D. Their central feature, now unsightly but once heavily decorated, was a platform for official appearances, which is known as the Bema and said to be the spot where Gallio acquitted St Paul; and, though it might be expected that a Roman governor would have heard cases in one of the basilicas, the visitor to this monument is often privileged to hear some devout pilgrim reciting to his party *Acts* 18, 1–17.

At the west end of the Roman Agora there stood the amusing monument of Babbius and several temples. The monument was a circle of eight Corinthian columns supporting an entablature and conical roof and resting on a rectangular podium; it was erected in the first century A.D. and pieces of it are lying near-by. The temples, of the first and second centuries A.D., were in the Roman manner set on high platforms with a flight of steps across the front. Behind are the West Shops, built early in the first century A.D. and restored in the fourth. Beyond was Temple E, also of the early first century A.D.: parts of its columns and entablature have been set up in front of the Museum, more conspicuously than they deserve.

The South Stoa was built soon after the middle of the fourth century B.C. It had at the front the regular outer Doric and inner Ionic colonnades, but the rear half of the stoa was divided into two storeys. The lower storey consisted of a row of taverns with front room, back room and backyard; there was a well in the front room and a simple latrine in the yard. Upstairs a corridor ran along the back and off it opened suites of ante-room and main room. The Roman colonists restored this stoa, but during the first century A.D. much of the rear part was remodelled for public offices. Shops of the original type survive at the west end, on the east side two sheds cover a Roman mosaic and a reconstructed part of the Greek roof, which explains better than any description the system of tiling.

7

Behind the South Stoa and entered through it are the ruins of the South Basilica, of about A.D. 40. At the front its main floor was about 10 feet above ground level, at the back it was set in a cutting. The basement was a wide corridor round a solid core. On the main floor a continuous aisle ran above the corridor and the central space was surrounded by Corinthian columns, which supported a clerestory. A flight of steps led up to a porch on the front side and there may have been another porch at the back. Basilicas of this type are known from other parts of the Roman world and could be used as markets or law courts. This one had no raised platform for a judge, though it contained statues of members of the Imperial family and other notables. The upper agora was closed at its east end by the South-East Building, the lower by the Julian Basilica, originally a twin of the South Basilica and also furnished with statues: they are of the same date as those of the South Basilica. Incidentally, these names (like most of the names of the buildings at Corinth) are modern.

On the east the lower agora overlooks the valley of Pirene. Above the fountain itself there was a stoa, next a monumental arched gateway, and to close the gap between the arch and the North-West Shops the Captives Facade, so-called because in its second storey colossal figures of barbarians (now in the Museum) took the place of columns. These buildings are all Roman and except for the stoa not early. The entrance to the basilica on the Lechaeum Road was through the Captives Facade.

Through what was the gateway a grand staircase descends to the Lechaeum Road. In Greek times this road turned off towards the west to enter the agora; the Romans made it a straight paved promenade, punctuated by steps and flanked by sidewalks and colonnades. Immediately on the right of the stairway as one goes down is the fountain of Pirene. The front of the fountain was remodelled time and again from the Archaic to the Early Byzantine period. The earliest significant remains are the three draw-basins about 9 feet in from the arches and the four long reservoirs behind them. In the late fourth century B.C. seven short walls were built forward and afterwards small Ionic columns were placed on the parapet of the old draw-basins. The Roman colonists put up the limestone wall with arches, which masks the Greek walls, and faced it with engaged Doric columns in a lower and Ionic in an upper storey. Next the court in front was enclosed by a similar wall and the sunken area made, where the water was delivered through pipes. The apses came with the remodelling of the second century A.D., perhaps paid for by Herodes Atticus, and the court was now completely done up with marble. Lastly, the clumsy colonnade across the front of the fountain was assembled in the fifth or sixth century from miscellaneous remains of earlier buildings.

North of Pirene is the Peribolos of Apollo, a large colonnaded court of the second century A.D. It was separated from the street by a row of shops, below the middle of which are the foundations of a small temple of the fourth century B.C. The area further north, past a Roman public lavatory with limestone seats, at least shows the continuity of the site: miserable Byzantine walls of various dates criss-cross the big Roman baths, and below in pits earlier levels have been disclosed. On the other side of the street, opposite the Peribolos, another row of Roman shops retained a terrace for the basilica which opened onto the Captives Facade. Below the basilica and on a different alignment there had been a market building of the fifth century B.C.: some of its stalls remain with traces of waterproof tanks on each side of their doors. The building to the north, into which a semi-circular colonnaded front has been inserted, was a Roman market.

On the north side of Temple Hill was the North Market, a colonnaded court with shops, built in the first century A.D. and rebuilt in Byzantine times. Its south side can be seen from the modern road, which crosses it. The Roman builders cut deeply into the hillside here and so removed most of the traces of a public bath, perhaps of the late fifth century B.C. Cuttings for this building, which was set obliquely to the market, can be seen at the south-east behind and at a higher level than the shops—a clear demonstration that the lowest level need not be the earliest. One tends to think of such amenities as baths as characteristically Roman, but they existed earlier though more modestly in Greece and the word 'thermae', used by the Romans for their baths, is in fact Greek. Further west there are the foundations of the North Stoa, built in the fifth century B.C.

Below the Museum one can look down into the Odeum, a small theatre which held an audience of about 3,000. The lower part is cut into the natural rock, the upper built up on concrete vaults. The Odeum was constructed in the late first century A.D., remodelled more showily by Herodes Atticus in the second century, rebuilt after a fire in the early third century and converted for gladiatorial shows and fights between hunters and wild beasts; to make more room for the performers and protect the spectators the lowest seats were cut away. Clumsy repairs of some later damage are visible in the stage building. The trapezoidal court behind the stage belongs to the second century A.D. Beyond the court was a Theatre, with an original capacity of about 18,000, which was built in the fourth century B.C. but altered more than once in Roman times. In some places the Greek seats survive below the Roman (which are steeper) and eventually the lowest rows were cut away as in the Odeum.

The sanctuary of Asklepios is a quarter of a mile north of the theatre. A path between the theatre and the excavators' dump (on which the Tourist Pavilion is boldly sited) leads to a hamlet near the scarp. A left turn in the hamlet brings one to the sanctuary, where a broken column has been set up as a landmark. The sanctuary was a rectangular enclosure round a small Doric temple, the plan of which is clear from cuttings in the rock. Near the entrance is an ancient offertory box. Though the temple was built only in the fourth century B.C. dedications buried about that time show that a healing god had been established there since the sixth century and, if (as is thought) the cult of Asklepios did not spread from Epidaurus till the late fifth century, Apollo is his likeliest predecessor. From the sanctuary a steep street goes down to the Corinthian Lerna, another rectangular court, surrounded by colonnades and with rooms behind on the east. These rooms were used for dining and one still has couches along the walls, slots for tables and in the middle the base of a hearth. The Greek custom at formal dinners and evening parties was for the men to recline on couches set against the walls and, though in private houses (as also in the dormitory at Brauron) the furniture was normally of wood, in public buildings one can understand the advantages of stone. At Lerna and in the sanctuary above there are also remains of the water system to puzzle out. Near-by what may be a Roman gymnasium is being excavated, and further west fragments of an outsize drum and architrave are evidence of a temple perhaps of the fifth century B.C. and at least 30 feet longer than that of Zeus at Olympia.

Just below Lerna there are traces of the city wall. The foundations of its outer face were at the foot of the scarp. Its inner face was set into the scarp itself and the space between was filled in with rubble and mudbrick. The top presumably was level with the court. Very little of the city wall survives or has been cleared, though its course is generally known. It starts on the west side of Acrocorinth, a little above the gates, runs west for nearly 300 yards to turn down north along a steep spur. After a mile or so it reaches the scarp above the coastal plain and continues eastwards along it for nearly 2 miles. Then it comes back south across the plateau to follow another spur up to the east side of Acrocorinth. A stretch of it can be seen, not preserved to much height, near the modern road to Old Corinth from the Argos highway; it is on the right, just before the crest of the road. The long walls which joined the city to the port of Lechaeum started one about 250 yards east of the sanctuary of Asklepios, the other from the north-east corner of the city circuit where a small part remains. So far as is known, these fortifications were constructed in the late fifth or early fourth century B.C., but except for the long walls had predecessors.

Not all the expanse within the walls was built up nor has much of it been explored. At the north-west corner there are poor ruins of a potters' quarter which was active from the eighth to the fourth century B.C. This was not the only place where potters worked, since kilns have been discovered and conserved about half a mile from the middle of the village of Old Corinth, where the road to the coast zig-zags down the scarp. About three quarters of a mile east of the village, above an upper scarp, what at first sight might be taken for a hollow is the lower part of an amphitheatre, a rarity east of the Adriatic. Its lower part was cut into the rock, the upper built up. The date is thought to be the third century A.D. Rather more than quarter of a mile south of the amphitheatre, across the track to Examilia and again just inside of the line of the city wall, a basilical church of the fifth century has been excavated. The ruins are low, but the plan is clear—nave, two aisles, narthex and a chapel for a martyr's tomb attached to the south aisle. The chapel has apses on its three free sides. Around the eleventh century a much smaller church was built over the ruins of the east part of the nave. There were several early churches at Corinth. As a big commercial centre it was more cosmopolitan than other cities of Roman Greece and more receptive. Finally, between the Agora and Acrocorinth a sanctuary of Demeter and Persephone existed from Archaic to Roman times; it appears from a distance as a scar on the hillside below the motor road to Acrocorinth.

The Museum, pleasant and well arranged, houses finds made in Corinth and the surrounding country, including the Isthmian Sanctuary and Nemea, but not Perachora or Sicyon. One room has the Prehellenic finds, a second the Greek (mainly pottery and terracottas), a third Roman and later (but mostly sculpture). More unusual are the contents of a fourth room, which one must ask the guard to open. These are replicas in terracotta of parts of the human body and were dedicated by patients in the sanctuary of Asklepios (or his predecessor). The same practice is to be seen in many Greek churches today, though now the

representations are stamped on little metal plaques and a new motif has
been substituted for cures of sterility. In the courtyard there are some
amusing Byzantine reliefs, and over the door leading to it a mosaic of
about 400 B.C., which depicts in black and white pebbles two griffins
attacking a horse. On its left a portrait of Herodes Atticus in the form
of a herm carries the inspiring message 'Herodes used to walk
here'.

Acrocorinth

The dominating hill of Acrocorinth, which rises to nearly 1,900 feet, is
worth visiting for its view and fortifications. The main entrance is at
the west and can be reached by a path from below the Museum or by a
fair road which connects with both the city site and the branch road to
the Argos highway. The walls of Acrocorinth are about 2 miles in
circumference and follow natural lines, and because of the height and
steepness of the approaches little modification was needed when
artillery developed. So though the superstructure is of various periods,
in most parts the foundations are Classical. No trace of any earlier,
Archaic wall has been identified so far, though one would expect that
Corinth had defences at that time and they could not have been effective
if Acrocorinth had been left out. Perhaps when the heavy Classical wall
was built, its predecessor was demolished completely. The Classical
wall was kept in repair till 146 B.C., when the Romans pulled parts of it
down and the rest was left to decay till in the fourth century A.D. the
menace of Barbarian invasions made it advisable to fortify cities once
more. In the sixth century, presumably, the Emperor Justinian restored
the defences, but it seems that they soon became derelict again. There
was another extensive restoration about the tenth century, and in 1205
Acrocorinth could resist a Frankish siege for five years (or forty-one
years, if the *Chronicle of the Morea* is to be believed). During the next
two and a half centuries—under the Franks, Florentine Acciajuoli, and
again Byzantines (with a short interregnum of the Knights of St John)—
the fortifications were generally maintained and even improved; but the
Turks, who arrived in 1458, soon let them decay, and though the Venetians repaired and modernised between 1687 and 1715, neglect returned
with the Turks. In 1822 the place was captured by Greek insurgents
and soon after was deserted completely. Acrocorinth was an expensive
fortress to keep up. Besides maintenance of the structure it needed a
garrison of at least 400 soldiers (supplemented in the third century B.C.

with fifty dogs and their keepers); about A.D. 1700 the Venetians reckoned that a thousand men were wanted, but then of course artillery had become more powerful.

Acrocorinth is a good place for comparing the styles of masonry of different periods and, even though specialists cannot distinguish them all precisely, some rough rules may be given. The ancient Greek work is of large squared blocks, carefully fitted without mortar. The Byzantine masons took any older materials that were at hand; at first they laid blocks regularly in courses, but later they incorporated miscellaneous architectural members, used smaller blocks and set them in mortar, and inserted thin bricks between. The Franks preferred small squared stones, set in mortar, but their usage varied. Turkish masonry is generally shoddier, imitating whatever model was available. The Venetians had higher standards, binding their ashlar or rubble with a strong mortar, and they often used a half-round moulding as a decorative feature. Still, whoever the architect, it must usually have been local workmen who did the building, and foreign styles were liable to be contaminated by native tradition.

The main entrance, where the hill is most open, was fortified in depth. One skirts the dry ditch, a Venetian addition once spanned by a movable wooden bridge, and comes to the first gate, which is basically Frankish; this too was not part of the original defences. The second gate is Middle Byzantine refaced by the Venetians, and the rest of the second entrance wall is of the same span of time. The third line is also largely Middle Byzantine and Venetian, though the facing of much of the tower to the right of the gate and of the far ends of the wall is the original Greek work. Inside the third gate a vast hollow rises ahead, with ruins of churches, mosques and houses (mostly Turkish) and below ground cisterns of various dates, whose open shafts—often masked by shrubs—are dangerous if one wanders off the path. The prominent building on the right is a Venetian magazine. Beyond the crest and to the left the path leads to the large house of—it is said—the Turkish commandant, pleasantly sited for an officer not too closely devoted to his duties. Just in front of this house is the spring of Upper Pirene, which an ancient fable asserted fed the Pirene in the lower city. In its existing form it has two underground chambers, reached by a flight of steps. The facade of the inner chamber may be of the third century B.C., as is its vault. A path along the south wall of the fortification goes to the west peak with its Frankish keep. The eastern and higher peak, due north of Upper Pirene, has a longer history. Here in ancient times was the neat but

unpretentious sanctuary of Aphrodite, notorious for its temple prosti-
tutes, not that the contemporary Greeks objected to more ordinary
prostitution. This made way in the fifth century A.D. for a Christian
church, which was remodelled more than once. Beside it was built a
large tower variously assigned to the sixth, tenth or thirteenth century—
a useful reminder of the uncertainties of archaeological chronology.
After the church there were successively two mosques and the Venetians
built a platform, generally said to be for artillery, though it does not look
as if it would have had a useful field of fire. Nothing of the Greek temple
is left in place, but its large blocks were re-used for all its successors.
The view from the peak is panoramic; even on a moderate day one can
see the snow of Parnassus and the smog of Athens. On the way back to
the main entrance, following the north wall, there is a postern gate,
constructed in early Byzantine times of older blocks. From here there is
a quick way down to the lower city, but not in sandals. For the more
active there is still the ascent (which very few make) of the hill of
Penteskouphi, $\frac{3}{4}$ mile south-west of Acrocorinth, or one can contemplate
it from the pleasant cafe outside the main entrance. Penteskouphi is
capped by a little Frankish fort built for the siege of Acrocorinth and so
securely dated between 1205 and 1210 (or 1246). Its curtain wall was
reconstructed at some later date to take cannons, though it is hard to
see why.

Lechaeum

Two miles north of Old Corinth, opposite the junction of the road from
the village and the road along the coast, two humps mark the site of the
ancient port of Lechaeum. Here Greek archaeologists have uncovered a
church dedicated to Bishop Leonidas and his seven virgins. The church
itself seems to have been built about A.D. 450 and its atrium around 520,
and the whole was destroyed by the earthquake of 551. Though the
ruins stand no more than 2 feet high, they are well preserved and there
are enough pieces of the superstructure around, so that the effect is
instructive as well as impressive. The church with its atrium was 610
feet long, nearly as big as St Peter's in Rome, and the quality of design
and workmanship was of metropolitan standard. It had nave with apse,
two aisles, rudimentary transept, narthex and exonarthex which opened
on to a grand semi-circular colonnade and a rectangular court. North of
the narthex was a detached complex consisting of an octagonal baptistery and a quatrefoil building which may have covered the martyr's

tomb. The walls were of rubble and brick, plastered over. Inside they were decorated with paintings or mosaics and the floor is still paved with coloured marble. The capitals, Corinthian and Ionic, are good work of their time. Unfortunately the rest of the site of Lechaeum is being improved with seaside chalets. Less than a mile east of the road junction an instructive Bronze Age site was excavated at Korakou.

Cenchreae

The other port, Cenchreae, was about 2 miles south of Isthmia, beside the new highway to Epidaurus. There is also a road from Examilia. Here the Americans have excavated buildings of the Roman period and more ruins show below the water. Some interesting glass panels have been brought up and pieces of veneering for furniture, but the site itself is not illuminating to the ordinary visitor.

The Isthmus

The sanctuary of Posidon on the Isthmus was famous for the Isthmian Games, held every two years and one of the four major athletic meetings of the Greek world. The site is towards the east side of the Isthmus, south of the canal, on the edge of the village of Kira Vrisi. The best roads to it branch off on the left side of the main road from the canal bridge to Corinth. It is easier to take the first, immediately after the bridge, and to turn sharp right in modern Isthmia on the road to Kira Vrisi (now named Oscar Broneer Street after the American excavator); almost at once Justinian's fort appears on the right and the sanctuary is beyond it, reaching up as far as the village school. Or one can take the next turn on the main road and go directly through Kira Vrisi.

The remains of the sanctuary are not spectacular, since most of the stone was carried off by Justinian's engineers. What can be made out are a large temple of the fourth century B.C., which had predecessors of the early fifth and mid seventh centuries, a remodelled Classical theatre, at the back of its auditorium two caves done up each as dining room with kitchen, and the end of a stadium. This stadium had an ingenious arrangement for starting the runners. Each bay has a socket for a post and a narrow channel that runs to a pit at the side of the track. Presumably each post had a hinged bar, held up by a cord that ran over and down the post and along the channel to a starter in the pit. In this way all the bars could be dropped simultaneously to release the competitors.

Ancient runners used a standing start (as did most of the sprinters in the first modern Olympiad) and the mechanism works. Later, but still in the Greek period, this stadium was remodelled and the starting line was put a little forward, but there are no signs here of a starting gate though one can see the two close-set grooves for the runners' feet. When the Games were re-established in the Roman period, a new site further to the south-east was chosen for the stadium and the old starting area became a precinct of Palaemon, one of those dim figures which students of Greek religion tend to think of as precursors of the Olympian gods, though curiously excavation has not yet revealed any sign of his cult before Roman times.

Justinian's fortress, the latest structure on the site, is quite well preserved. It was built, as much as possible of older materials, towards the middle of the sixth century A.D. as part of the defensive wall across the Isthmus to keep out the Slavs. Another piece of this wall stands at the side of the main road from the canal bridge to Corinth, opposite the turn for Kira Vrisi. There are remains too of an unrecorded Mycenaean wall, of the end of the thirteenth century B.C., plainly visible just beyond Isthmia on the right side of the road to Cenchreae. According to records walls across the Isthmus were built or restored in 480 and 279 B.C., A.D. 253, the sixth century, 1396 and 1415. They were never of much use; the terrain is not too helpful and the position can be turned by sea.

A more successful trans-Isthmian construction was the Diolkos, a carefully graded roadway for hauling ships across from one shore to the other. It was in existence in the sixth century B.C., and is said to have been used as late as the ninth century A.D. A good stretch can be examined on either side of the coastal road from Corinth to Loutraki, just before the ferry. Here the Diolkos is cut into the rock, with two ruts for the wheels of the carrier on which the ship sat. In ancient times only the Emperor Nero, in A.D. 67, seriously planned a canal, but he did not live to complete it and his cuttings disappeared when the modern canal was made in the late nineteenth century.

Perachora

The promontory of Perachora, the ancient Peiraion, is conspicuous in any view north from Corinth. Near its tip, about 200 yards short of the light-house, there is a tiny harbour with the remains of an ancient sanctuary of Hera, which British archaeologists dug in the early 1930's with more luck than skill. The small finds, which include besides pottery and terracotta figurines some excellent bronzes and ivories and interesting terracotta models of temples of around 700 B.C., are mostly in the National Museum at Athens, though a batch of mediocre objects have been brought back to the little museum in Perachora village. From Loutraki (about 4 miles north of the bridge over the canal) a road winds up to this village and there turns left for the Heraeum (Ireon), skirting a lagoon and after 12 miles finishing above the harbour; the last part of this road is roughish, though passable. By the harbour there are from left to right remains of an L-shaped two-storeyed stoa of the late fourth century B.C., an altar with four—originally eight—column bases round it (probably to support a canopy), a temple of the later sixth century B.C., and a squarish colonnaded enclosure known as the 'Agora' but of unknown purpose. Going back up the gully, beyond the chapel (which houses a dubious portion of St John the Fasting) one passes a cistern with well designed internal supports and alongside it a dining room (as at the Asklepieion in Corinth and at the Isthmian sanctuary). In the little plain between the head of the gully and the lagoon there are traces of houses and some well preserved deep cisterns. Though the sanctuary goes back at least to the eighth century, most of these remains seem to be of around 300 B.C. The sanctuary was justified by the harbour, which gave shelter against strong north winds, but it is harder to explain the settlement, since there is no spring in all this part of the promontory and indeed the excavators used to ferry water across from the other side of the gulf. The ruins of the Heraeum are not impressive, but the place is picturesque with its trees and rocks, though the appropriate solitude is not to be found at week-ends.

Sicyon

Sicyon, 10 miles away, was Corinth's neighbour on the west. It too had its strip of fertile plain, of which the main part was about 5 miles long by 2 wide, and though not much interested in the sea became fairly prosperous and was famous for its long line of sculptors and painters. About the middle of the seventh century B.C. an unusually successful tyranny was established and lasted for a hundred years till it was suppressed by the Spartans. In 303 B.C. Demetrius Poliorcetes, one of the Macedonian competitors for the empire left by Alexander the Great, captured Sicyon and is said to have shifted the city further inland, though there seems already to have been some inhabitation of the area round the Museum, and sixty years or so later it became the leading member of the anti-Macedonian Achaean League. In 146 B.C., when Corinth was destroyed by the Romans, Sicyon inherited the Corinthian territory and the Isthmian Games, but had to give them back in 44 B.C. when Corinth was refounded. After an earthquake in the third century A.D. the survivors moved to a site near the coast at what is now called Kiato.

The earliest Sicyon has not been explored nor indeed located precisely, but Greek and American excavators have uncovered part of Demetrius's city. This straddles a side road, duly signposted, which runs inland from the highway to Patras, climbing a steep scarp and passing through the village of Vasiliko. About half a mile on and to the right one cannot miss the Museum, an attractive reutilisation of the red-brick ruins of some Roman baths. Straight ahead is a theatre, built in the third century B.C. and remodelled later. To its right the shape of the stadium can be made out from the cutting and embankment for it. On the other side of the theatre and across the road is a gymnasium on two levels; both the upper and the lower court had colonnades on three sides and the retaining wall between is enlivened by an elegantly balanced arrangement of three staircases and two fountains. Seventy yards further down a square building with internal columns served as the Council House of the Achaean League, and beyond it there was a stoa more than a hundred yards along. Between the Council House and the Museum the foundations of a temple have been uncovered, unusually long and narrow for its period. All these buildings are thought to be of the third or second century B.C. and, when more has been excavated, we may have a good example of Hellenistic town-planning. The hill above the theatre provided the acropolis, a sizable plateau with a few blocks of its wall still in place. The Museum, cool and agreeable, has some important figured mosaics of black and white pebbles, as early as the fourth century B.C., some sculpture—most of it Roman—and the modest contents of graves of the earliest city, which show that from the beginning painted pottery was imported from Corinth. Sicyon is a minor site and lacks shade, but especially after Corinth it is refreshingly deserted.

Nemea

The sanctuary of Nemea, where Heracles killed the lion, was in the territory of Cleonae, annexed by Argos around 450 B.C. From Corinth one climbs the main road south (which goes on to Argos) until it reaches the final crest at Nemea Station, where wayside stalls sell a tonic wine called Heracles' Blood and credibly drawn from a tyrant's vein, though some find it condoling. A little past the station a side road on the right leads to both ancient and modern Nemea. To ancient Nemea, at modern Iraklion, is 3 miles. The sanctuary lies on the right, just before the village, and it was here that the Nemean Games (one of the premier Greek festivals) were held every two years from 573 B.C., when they were founded, till the middle of the third century B.C., when they were transferred—perhaps not permanently—to Argos. Excavation has been done on the site at various times by the French and the Americans, but never comprehensively.

The chief monument is the temple of Zeus, of which three columns, most of the platform and part of the bottom course of the cella walls are still in place. This temple was built around the middle of the fourth century B.C. and is one of the important Doric temples of its time. If one remembers the fifth century temples of Athens, it is clear that the Doric canon has been modified: at Nemea the columns are slenderer and their number on the sides was reduced to twelve for a front of six. The interior colonnade had Corinthian capitals. In some details there is a close resemblance to the temple at Tegea, and the two buildings might be by the same architect. The altar, opposite the entrance ramp, is almost as long as the temple. To the south some confusing ruins have been exposed. Those near the shed that houses finds are from a bath, and to the east there was a long hotel; both are of the fourth or early third century B.C. In the fifth century A.D. a basilical church was built over part of the site of the hotel; it had an apsidal nave, two aisles, a narthex, and a baptistery. Finally, the stadium and a theatre can be detected as hollows on the hillside to the east, but nothing more substantial remains.

6 · The Argolid and Epidaurus

The Argolid (*Fig.* 13) was in ancient times the plain of Argos and the hilly country round as far as the watersheds. To the east its neighbours were the territories of Hermione at the end of the gulf and of Troizen and Epidaurus along the Aegean coast. There is a main road from Corinth to Argos, which goes on past Lerna to Tripolis; another good road leads from Argos past Tiryns to Nauplia and Epidaurus; and a new highway is being made from the Isthmus past Cenchreae to Epidaurus. Other sites are served by side roads, some of them fair. For most visitors Nauplia is the best place to stay at, but Epidaurus though remoter has its attractions and Tolo a camping site.

The plain of Argos was one of the largest and most fertile of ancient Greece and inhabited from the earliest times. In the Late Bronze Age Mycenae was to all appearances its most important site and is commonly believed (though without proof) to have subjected the rest of the Argolid. Of the Early Iron Age we know very little, but by the Archaic period Argos had become the principal city, always ready to annex its neighbours, and it has kept its primacy, even if on occasions of naval activity Nauplia was more valuable strategically. Epidaurus, Troizen and Hermione, though independent in the Hellenic era, were and always have been too small to be significant.

Mycenae   (*Fig.* 14, *Plate* 8)

The usual approach to Mycenae (Mikini) is from the Corinth-Argos highway, turning off 5 miles from Argos by a side road to the east, which goes through the modern village, passes the Treasury of Atreus, and after $2\frac{1}{2}$ miles ends at the car park opposite the citadel. This citadel occupies a small hill at the north-east corner of the Argive plain and is now remote, and though in ancient times one of the routes from Corinth to Argos went past it and there was a way behind to Berbati its situation was strong rather than strategic. Nor had it a natural supply of water. Even so, to Homer Mycenae 'rich in gold' was the senior kingdom of

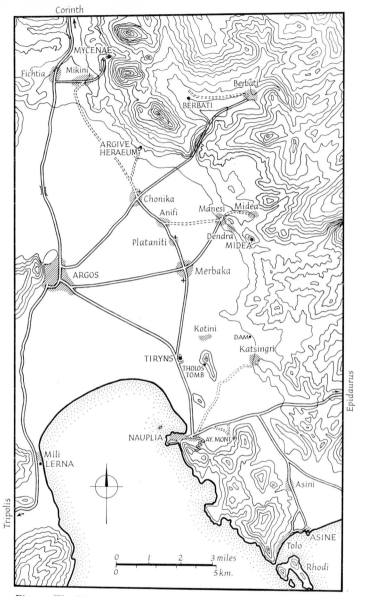

Fig. 13. The Plain of Argos.
Contours at 50 metre intervals. ● ancient site. + Byzantine church.

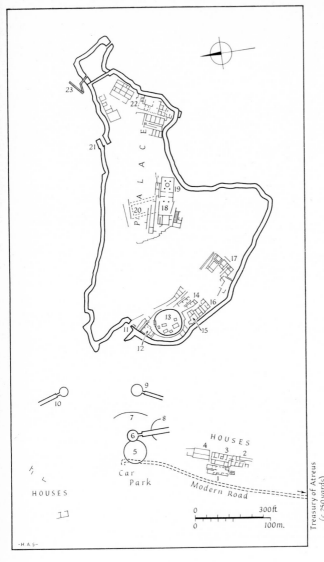

Fig. 14.

Mycenae, the citadel

1, West House.
2, House of Sphinxe[s]
3, House of Oil Merchant.
4, House of Shields.
5, Grave Circle B.
6, Tomb of Clytemnestra.
7, Retaining wall fo[r] mound over 6.
8, Hellenistic Theat[re]
9, Tomb of Aegisth[us]
10, Lion Tomb.
11, Lion Gate.
12, Granary.
13, Grave Circle A.
14, Ramp House
15, House of Warrio[r] Vase.
16, South House.
17, Tsountas's Hous[e]
18, Palace court.
19, Palace 'megaron'
20, Hellenistic Temp[le]
21, Postern Gate.
22, House of Colum[ns]
23, Secret Cistern.

Plate 8. Air view of the citadel of Mycenae from the west.

Heroic Greece and its legends of Atreus, Agamemnon and Clytemnestra
have become immortal. With its romantic aspect, especially in the shifting light of showery weather, Mycenae makes a stronger impression
than any other mainland site on those who like the past to have a barbaric
and mysterious grandeur, though some of the mystery has rubbed off
with the decipherment of the Linear B tablets. According to the archaeologists, whose reconstruction of the history of the site is far from final,
the hill of Mycenae became important about the sixteenth century B.C.,
when the palace area was fortified. The extension of the citadel and the
big houses outside the wall belong to the fourteenth and early thirteenth
centuries and made Mycenae the largest known community of

contemporary Greece. About 1250 B.C. some limited conflict destroyed the suburbs and part of the citadel, and in the next century in spite of improved defences the citadel too was overwhelmed in the general disasters of the time. Though there was a partial recovery, Mycenaean Mycenae had ended by 1100 B.C. During the Early Iron Age the site was occupied in a humble way and a small independent city developed, which fought at Plataea and was suppressed by Argos in the 460's. A new city was founded in the third century B.C., but by the second century A.D. (when Pausanias paid his visit) the site had been deserted for ever. Though the name slipped out of local memory and the Albanian village that grew up lower down the slope was called Charvati, the ancient remains were conspicuous enough to be recognised and described by educated travellers. Fittingly, the first excavation was left for the sympathetic Schliemann (1874–6), and his work has been continued more cautiously by Greek and British archaeologists, notably Wace. The finds are divided between Athens and Nauplia, but the most spectacular are in Athens.

The present wall round the citadel goes back in the main to the mid fourteenth century B.C. It runs irregularly, taking advantage of the slope, was built of enormous roughly hewn blocks of limestone with a rubble core, had a thickness of 18 feet or more, and presumably was crowned with a walk and parapet. The two gates and their approaches, thoughtfully designed to expose attackers to cross-fire, are faced with large squared blocks of conglomerate and may be later improvements. In the second half of the thirteenth century a small extension was made at the east, with access to a new supply of water (the 'Secret Cistern'); previously the citadel had depended on the collection of rainwater; now terracotta pipes tapped a spring 400 yards further east and emptied into an underground chamber outside the wall, but accessible by a stairway from inside. (This stairway, with a hundred winding steps, needs candles or torches.) In various parts of the circuit patches of smaller, often polygonal stones show later, mainly Hellenistic, repairs, but it is harder to detect the extensive modern restorations. Against the assaults of its time—javelins, arrows, sling-stones, hooks, ladders and (where the ground permitted) rams—the fortifications of Mycenae should have been impregnable, if properly manned. Even so, though in part they acted also as a retaining wall, they were uneconomical structurally. Labour must have been plentiful and cheap.

The Lion Gate is still the main entrance. It gets its name from the carved slab, best lighted in the evening, which closes the triangular relieving space above the lintel. The heads of the lions (or lionesses), now lost, were made separately and perhaps of finer material. The beasts rear up against a column, but the significance of the subject is any-one's guess. This is our largest specimen of Mycenaean sculpture. Cuttings in the jambs and threshold show how the wooden doors were fixed.

Inside, towards the right, is Grave Circle A, which encloses Schlie-mann's famous shaft graves. There were six of them, containing nineteen bodies. The rich furnishings, which included the clumsy gold masks (not in the strict sense death masks) and the elegant inlaid daggers, are in Athens. These graves are of the sixteenth century B.C and belonged to the Prehistoric Cemetery, which may have extended as far as the other Grave Circle. When the citadel was enlarged, the new wall cut across this cemetery, but these shaft graves were respected. A retaining wall was built on the south side and the ground raised to the height of the surviving parapet. Inside, the ineptly carved gravestones were set up again at the new level. Round about, as elsewhere on the citadel, there are ruins of Mycenaean houses, some of them three storeys high. The palace is at the top of the hill. It was built in the mid four-teenth century, obliterating the palace of the shaft graves and itself partly obliterated at the south by natural erosion and at the north by an Archaic temple, which in turn was supplanted by the Hellenistic temple, still traceable by its foundations. Recently the south side of the main suite of the later palace and still more of its megaron have been rebuilt, perhaps correctly; all the same the palace of Mycenae can be understood more easily after a visit to Tiryns or still better to Pylos.

Beyond the palace a path leads down to the eastern extension. Here there are on the north the Secret Cistern and a culvert and at the south-east a doorway opening on to a natural platform above the ravine. It is curious that this platform, which blocks the view from the wall, was not included in the fortified area. Going back along the north wall one comes to the postern gate, below which a quiet track offers an excellent view of the whole of the wall and beyond it passes above the Tomb of the Lions, a neat but topless tholos near the ticket office. There is one cau-tion about this track; though it goes round behind the entrance to the citadel and the car park, there may be no way through the perimeter fence except for chance holes.

Here and there outside the citadel are burial places and clusters of well-to-do houses. Burials have by their nature an unusually good chance of survival, so that archaeology tends to over-emphasise the

importance of death. The Mycenaeans practised interment, not crema-
tion, and there were three main types of sepulchre. Graves, of which the
royal shaft graves are a richer variety, were universal in the early period
and continued for the poor. Later, the wealthier preferred rectangular
chamber-tombs cut into the soft rock and entered by a sloping passage
(or 'dromos'). These were family vaults and when a new interment was
made bones of earlier occupants were swept unceremoniously out of the
way. For royalty, which wanted something bigger, the tholos (or bee-
hive) tomb was devised, an underground structure shaped like the
pointed half of an egg. Nine of these are known at Mycenae, dating from
about 1500 to 1300 B.C. The method of construction was to dig a pit in
the hillside, lay the courses of masonry within it, back them with clay,
and fill in behind with earth and rubble. The entrance ('dromos') was a
wide horizontal cutting from the edge of the hill. The earliest tholos
tombs (such as the 'Tomb of Aegisthus') were built of rubble, the latest
(like the 'Treasury of Atreus') of deep blocks with neatly finished faces.
The inward curve of the wall was produced by corbelling, since the
principle of the arch was not known; each course of stones projected a
little forward of the one below, jammed in position by small stones and
clay, and the apex was capped with a large flat stone. It is not surprising
that most tholos tombs have collapsed. Often they contained several
burials, and after each occasion the door was walled up and the dromos
filled with earth. The furnishing of Mycenaean burials was proportion-
ate to the station of the deceased, but since tholos tombs are not easily
concealed they were almost always robbed. A few of them were venerated by the later Greeks as tombs of Heroes (the ancient equivalent of
Saints), though visitors must not be misled by the modern names, which
are arbitrary and do not even fit the legendary dates of the characters
they are named after.

Outside the Lion Gate is the tholos tomb called the 'Tomb of Aegisthus', of the early fifteenth century B.C. Beyond it is the 'Tomb of
Clytemnestra', built near 1300 B.C. and recently restored. It encroaches
on Grave Circle B, a group of shaft graves found in 1951 within the
curve of the modern road, rather earlier than Schliemann's but much
less rich and more quickly forgotten. By the Hellenistic period the
'Tomb of Clytemnestra' too had passed out of memory, and the seats of
a theatre were built across its dromos. Still finer is the 'Treasury of
Atreus', of the late fourteenth century, about a quarter of a mile down
the road. This is the largest of the tholos tombs and abnormally has a
side chamber. We also know more of its decoration. Outside, the great

doorway was flanked by engaged columns of a green stone, carved with horizontal zig-zags; and there were similar but smaller columns above them, framing the relieving triangle, which once was closed (as in the Lion Gate) and crossed by bands of spirals in a reddish stone. Parts of the larger columns were brought to England by Lord Elgin and are in the British Museum, fragments of the rest are in Athens. Inside, holes in the walls once supported bronze ornaments. The smoke stains at the top are the vestiges not of religious rites, but of shepherds' fires through the long centuries when the tomb was half filled with earth and used as a casual shelter.

The view from Mycenae is instructive. To the south is the conical citadel of Argos, further left the low hump of Tiryns and behind it the peninsula of Nauplia. Five miles further on, but out of sight, was Asine near the modern Tolo. All these were considerable Mycenaean sites and afterwards independent Greek cities, till between the eighth and fifth centuries B.C. Argos swallowed up the others. What is also illuminating is that the full prospect can be enjoyed from the car park opposite the Lion Gate, but from nowhere within the citadel can one see Nauplia or Tiryns.

In the village the inn called 'la Belle Hélène' is now almost a place of literary pilgrimage, though there is not so much of the original structure left.

Tiryns   (*Fig.* 15)

The citadel of Tiryns, on an outcrop of limestone which rises to 60 feet above the plain, is on the left of the road from Argos to Nauplia, about 5 miles from Argos and 3 from Nauplia. Because of its defensibility it was already a centre of settlement in the Neolithic Age and, as at Mycenae, a fortified palace arose in the late sixteenth century B.C. In the mid fourteenth century the area was levelled, the palace improved or rebuilt, and the wall extended to the south. The settlement outside, which seems to have been less wealthy than that of Mycenae, was destroyed about 1250. Although the citadel was strengthened with extra fortifications (now enclosing the northern, lower half of the hill) and with a bigger palace, it too was taken and burnt early in the twelfth century. Soon afterwards there was some modest rebuilding, but hardly a revival. There are signs of occupation in the Early Iron Age and of a sanctuary of the early and a temple of the late seventh century B.C., when Tiryns was a small independent state. Again like Mycenae it

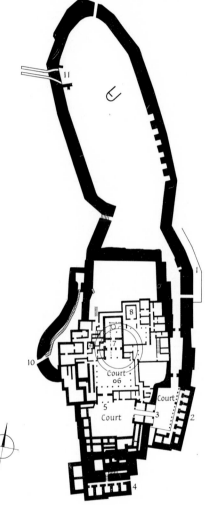

Fig. 15.

Tiryns, the Citadel.

1, entrance ramp.

2, passage and rooms in wall.

3, propylon.

4, passage and rooms in wall.

5, propylon.

6, altar.

7, principal 'megaron'; the walls shown by a broken line are of a later replacement, and the circle gives the position of a much earlier structure.

8, small 'megaron'.

9, bathroom.

10, postern.

11, concealed stairways to springs.

0   150 ft

0   50 m.

fought at Plataea and was destroyed by Argos in the 460's. Pausanias found the place deserted in the second century A.D. In the Middle Byzantine period a small church (of which nothing remains now) was put up at the south end of the hill and after its collapse the citadel was left again to shepherds.

Excavation began in 1884 with Schliemann and his more conscientious assistant Dörpfeld. Later the German School worked more intensively on the southern part of the citadel, but since—naturally enough—they did not demolish any substantial remains of the late palace our understanding of earlier periods is very patchy and the summary given in the last paragraph should not be taken as gospel. The northern half of the citadel and the settlement outside have not yet been explored systematically, though recently the Greeks have restored much of the walls and made some incidental and interesting discoveries. The finds are divided unequally between Athens and Nauplia.

Though the stones are bigger than those of Mycenae, it is not till one is very close that the fortifications of Tiryns become impressive. They are of two periods, most of the present external wall being late, and about 20 feet thick. The main approach is on the east, on the side away from the sea, up a broad ramp commanded by the wall. At the top is the outer gateway, which at some time (whether during or after the Mycenaean Age) was partly blocked up; though there are no cuttings to take doors, it is incredible that this entry was left open. Inside, a passage runs along the wall in both directions. Northward one goes down to the lower part of the hill, usually thought to have been fortified as the place of refuge for the inhabitants of the country around or perhaps for the lord's livestock, though at some time it contained permanent houses. Near the far end of its west wall, much as at Mycenae, two concealed stairways lead to underground springs just outside. Southwards from the main gateway the passage leads up through two more gates (the first of which was at one time the main outer entrance) into an irregular court with a colonnade on the left. Behind the colonnade and at a lower level there was a narrow passage with rooms opening off it, all constructed with corbelled ceilings within the thickness of the wall: the tops and ends of the rooms have collapsed, but the passage is still complete, with its walls polished in their lower part by the rubbing of innumerable sheep. At the south end of the citadel is a similar construction, with rooms (but not passage) better preserved.

With the court the civil part of the citadel begins. The threatening grimness of the fortifications is still palpable, but it needs effort to

imagine the cheerful luxury of the palace, since its ruins hardly anywhere
stand more than 2 feet high. The entrance is through a deep double
porch, like a Classical propylon (even to the columns on both fronts)
though, since this is an obvious design for an ornamental gateway, the
similarity is probably accidental. Beyond is another large court, with
store rooms to the south and on the north another but smaller propylon.
Through this propylon one comes out in the corner of a third and more
regular court, which has colonnades on three sides, a round altar centrally on the south, and opposite it the porch of the principal suite or,
as it is called conventionally, the 'megaron'. Essentially a megaron is a
longish house consisting of a porch and behind it a squarish room, which
should have a hearth in the middle; and though this is a structurally
obvious type of simple house, many archaeologists like to believe it a
sign of Northern immigrants and the ancestor of the Greek temple.
Here the porch and the main room were separated by a shallow ante-
room, entered (as in the Minoan architecture of Crete) by three doors
in its front wall in correspondence with the two columns of the porch.
The main room had a large circular hearth in the centre and round it
four columns supporting the roof and perhaps some sort of projecting
lantern to let out the smoke without letting in the rain. The floor was
stuccoed and decorated in squares containing dolphins, octopods or net
pattern, set to face the right wall, against the middle of which a large
rectangle was marked off by its different decoration, presumably to give
dignity to a throne. The walls too were painted—one of the subjects was
a modishly vigorous boar hunt, a large fragment of which is on show in
Athens. The narrow wall that runs along the megaron rather left of
centre was built later, after the destruction of the palace, and belongs to
a building that made use of the east wall of the megaron for its own east
wall: though often considered an Archaic temple, it is probably an
impoverished replacement of the megaron put up in the twelfth century
B.C.

On the east of this megaron is a complex of buildings, of which the
most important is a smaller and less elaborate megaron opening on to
its own courtyard. Its only access is by long passages from a side door
in the first propylon and from the domestic rooms to the west of the big
megaron. Because of its seclusion some archaeologists call the east
complex the queen's apartments; others think it was meant for a prince
or distinguished guests. The purpose of the west rooms also is obscure,
except for the bathroom. This has for its floor a single slab of stone,
tilted slightly to drain through a cavity on the east side. To judge by

peg holes in the floor the walls were lined. The excavators found pieces of a terracotta tub in this room. Stumps of staircases showed that there were upper storeys in this part of the palace.

In its planning the palace is a mixture of the symmetrical and the casual. For example in the courtyard of the big megaron, where particular care was given to formal correspondence, the propylon was unnecessarily in a corner. Published restorations show the roof levels as up and down, but this is quite conjectural. The complex on the west side had at least two storeys, and the big megaron is thought to have had only one, but that was probably very high. The method of construction (according to the excavators) was to lay foundations of stone of which the top course was carefully squared, and to carry the walls up in timber and mudbrick, though the example of Pylos suggests that the change of material may have been at the level of the first floor. Columns were of wood on a round stone base. The roofs were flat, presumably of timber covered with stamped or rolled clay. Walls, inside and out, and floors were stuccoed and, if reckoned worth it, painted with scenes or patterns.

This palace was built about 1250 and, since it lasted only a couple of generations, shows little or no evidence of modification. We know hardly anything of its predecessor or predecessors, though remains of wall paintings suggest a general similarity in style. Of still earlier structures the most substantial was a round building over 90 feet across with a double wall of stone, buttressed outside, and a tiled roof. It is datable rather before 2200 B.C., of unknown purpose and unique. It lay partly under the big megaron, but its remains have been covered up again.

Behind the palace is a large open space, strongly fortified; before the northern enclosure was taken in, this was the outer defence to the north. On its west is a bastion, from which a great wall, built up from the foot of the hill, swings round to the south. Within it a staircase leads down to a postern gate not far from a spring, but its main purpose may have been the convenience of the occupants of the palace; it is too cramped to have been of much military use.

Tiryns too has a tholos tomb, on a hillside about $\frac{3}{4}$ mile east of the citadel; it is badly preserved. More interesting, though as a work of engineering and not of art, is a dam of great blocks of stone about $\frac{1}{2}$ mile north of Katsingri, $2\frac{1}{2}$ miles east of Tiryns. Its purpose is thought to have been to divert flood water from the town that stood below the citadel and, if so, it has been permanently successful. How big this town was has still to be discovered, but it seems to have been more compact than the extra-mural settlement at Mycenae.

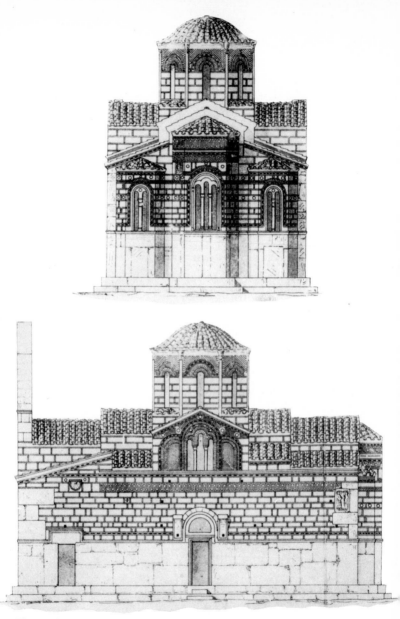

Plate 9. Church of the Panayia at Merbaka, east and south elevations.

Fig. 16. Merbaka, church of the Panayia: section and plan (cf. *Plate* 9).
(A. Struck in *Athenische Mitteilungen* xxxiv, pl. 10.2 and 1).

It is often asserted that Tiryns was subordinate to Mycenae and served as its port. At present Tiryns is a good mile from the sea, and though in ancient times it may have been nearer, the shore must have been open and probably marshy. Besides, the gate of the citadel is on the landward side and Nauplia with its good harbourage is close enough. As for the political relationship between Mycenae and Tiryns, Greek legend (for what it is worth) has an independent kingdom of Tiryns and its palace was certainly very rich and large for a vassal. Another question the visitor must decide for himself is why the Mycenaean fortifications were built—for protection from foreigners or neighbouring lords or from the local population. It is surprising how much is uncertain about Mycenaean life, and to avoid extra confusion it is well to emphasise that when archaeologists and historians use the word 'Mycenaean' they are referring not specifically to Mycenae, but to the whole civilisation of which Mycenae was the most famous centre; Mycenaean pottery, for instance, was made at Athens and in Rhodes as well as in the Argolid.

The Eastern Argolid

Between Tiryns and Mycenae there are several minor but interesting sites and monuments. The roads to them meet at Chonika, one starting

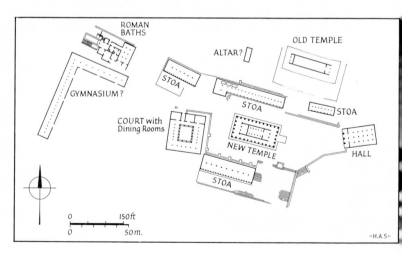

Fig. 17. The Argive Heraeum.

at Tiryns (just west of the ruins) and continuing as a track—in part roughish—to Mycenae village, the other coming from Argos and going on through the hills to Berbati (now officially called Prosymna).

The church of the Panayia at *Merbaka* or, as it has been renamed, Ayia Triadha (*Fig.* 16, *Plate* 9) is about 3 miles from Tiryns on the road to Chonika. It stands on the left of the road, a little before the village, in an exuberant graveyard and is a remarkably fine and well preserved example of the Middle Byzantine style of southern Greece, having lost externally not much more than the cornice below the roof of the dome and gained in the fifteenth or sixteenth century the incongruous belfry at its west end. The plan is characteristic of its period and the decoration of the outside rich but well controlled. Ancient marble blocks have been re-used for the three-stepped platform (which recalls that of the Doric temple) and for the lower courses and the corners of the walls, and above there is the familiar cloisonné masonry of limestone and brick. The broad ornamental bands have abstract patterns that succeed the Cufic seen in Athens. Earlier reliefs are displayed judiciously, and—especially at the east end—glazed bowls are inserted in the fabric. Inside, the dome is supported by four well proportioned columns, whose capitals show their descent from ancient forms, but the paintings which originally covered the walls and ceilings have vanished or been washed over. Above the lesser south door there is a Byzantine sundial. There is a close resemblance in style between the three neighbouring churches of Chonika, Ayia Moni and Merbaka, which appear to have been built in that order. Since Ayia Moni is dated to the 1140's, Merbaka should be of the second half of the twelfth or the early thirteenth century.

In *Plataniti*, the next village on the road to Chonika, one passes on the right a diminutive church of the Saviour, simpler in style and plan and much repaired and restored. It was built probably in the early twelfth century, though the paintings inside are later. In *Chonika* itself there is a larger church of the Dormition, which should be compared with Merbaka. The decoration is severer and perhaps less harmonious. As in some eleventh-century Greek churches big marble crosses are set into the outer walls. Its date is probably the early twelfth century, though the belfry was added later and there has been much restoration.

For the *Argive Heraeum* (*Fig.* 17) one leaves Chonika by the track to Mycenae and very soon forks right along a roughish track till in a mile or so it stops at the foot of a small hill. This hill, often identified as the ancient Prosymna, was inhabited throughout the Bronze Age and had a fair-sized Mycenaean settlement. Later, about the middle of the eighth

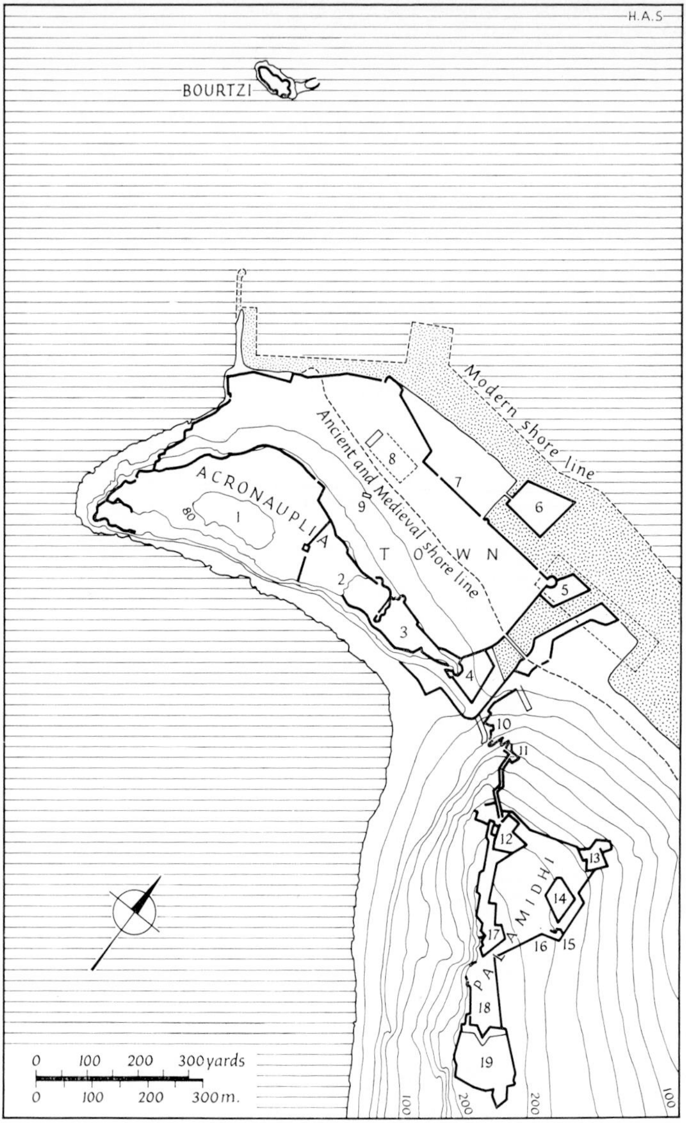

Fig. 18. **Nauplia.** 1, Castle of the Greeks. 2, Castle of the Franks. 3, Toron castle. 4, Grimani bastion. 5, Venetian bastion (now demolished): the long rectangle drawn with broken lines is the modern square north of the railway station. 6, Venetian ravelin (now demolished). 7, Venetian sea wall (now demolished). 8, Museum and Syntagma Square. 9, Ay. Sophia. 10, steps. 11, Fort Robert. 12, Fort Andreas. 13, Fort Leonidas. 14, Fort Miltiades. 15, Fort Epaminondas. 16, main gate of Palamidhi. 17, Fort Themistocles. 18, Fort Achilles. 19, Turkish extension (Fort Phocion).

Contours at 20 metre intervals. Stippling shows land reclaimed since Venetian and Turkish times.

century B.C., a sanctuary of Hera grew up near the foot and although nearly 5 miles from Argos itself it became the principal holy place of the Argive plain. The elder General Gordon dug here in 1836, but the main excavation has been American and the plan of the site is now clear, though the remains are not spectacular. The lower terrace was reached by a very wide stairway. In the middle was the temple, at the east a hall with internal columns, along the north side stoas, and at the west a squarish building with a court inside and dining rooms. Most of these structures were of the sixth or fifth century B.C., though the long stoa on the north goes back to the late seventh. On the terrace above there are the very meagre remains of a big earlier temple, built perhaps in the seventh century and burnt down in 423 B.C. Further west and at a lower level remains can be seen of—perhaps—a gymnasium and of Roman baths. The finds are in the National Museum at Athens.

Berbati (officially Prosymna) is about 5 miles from Chonika in a little plain beyond the hills. About 2 miles west of the village there is a conspicuous conical hill with remains of a Mycenaean town, excavated by the Swedes. This hill is not more than fifteen minutes walk from the road as it enters the plain, or one can go on to the modern village and turn back left along a roughish track, which passes near the site and continues as a path to Mycenae. The ruins, now more evocative than instructive, are on the south side of the hill and there is a small tholos tomb to the north-east.

Nauplia

(*Fig.* 18)

Nauplia has an old-fashioned provincial charm that is not Greek or at least is not found elsewhere on the Greek mainland. This is due to its fortunate periods of expansion and stagnation, but may not survive the development that successful tourism brings. Even so, Nauplia is likely to remain the best centre from which to visit the antiquities of the Argolid.

The peninsula on which the old castle and town stood used to be both narrower and more detached. All the low ground on its north side is Venetian or later reclamation, and the approach along the foot of Palamidhi was once not much more than 20 yards wide. Though there has been no systematic excavation, various finds show that people were living in this area before the end of Neolithic times. In the Early Iron Age Nauplia was an independent Greek city, which Argos conquered in the late seventh century B.C. but preserved as a useful port. Presumably the citadel (Acronauplia or Itch Kale) was fortified then, though the earliest wall now visible is only of about 300 B.C. Visitors in the Roman period found the site deserted, but perhaps no later than the third and fourth centuries A.D. the defences were restored and modernised. They were again in good order at the beginning of the thirteenth century, when the Byzantine representatives held out against the Franks till 1210 (or 1247 according to the *Chronicle of the Morea*) and were reduced only by a naval blockade. The Venetians bought the fortress in 1388 and in the later fifteenth century adapted it for artillery warfare, but after resisting several sieges had to cede it to the Turks in 1540. By now there was a considerable town on the north side of the citadel and Nauplia became the capital of the province of the Peloponnese, but in spite of the increasing range of cannons the Turks neglected to fortify the hill of Palamidhi, which overlooks Acronauplia. So in 1686 the Venetians bombarded the fortress from above till it surrendered and in their second occupancy built the upper defences. Yet impregnable though Nauplia now seemed, in 1715 it fell to the Turks after only ten days attack, perhaps through treachery rather than the weakness of the garrison. After a century of neglect it was captured in 1822 by the Greek insurgents and from 1828 till 1834 was the capital of free Greece. Since then much of the old town has been destroyed, not altogether in the interest of progress. The general design of the fortress of Acronauplia can be appreciated most easily from Palamidhi. It is in three parts—the Castle of the Greeks at the west, the Castle of the Franks in the middle, and the Toron Castle at the landward eastern end. The first two of these parts form the ancient citadel, and their division dates from the Frankish occupation. On the south the steepness of the cliff made artificial defences unnecessary, on the west and north the present wall follows the ancient line and in some places the Greek foundations can be seen from outside, where they are not covered by a sloping Venetian talus, but the upper parts are of various periods. The biggest changes were at the short east end, since both the approach and the entrance were there. This stretch of wall was reinforced in late Roman or Medieval times by three semi-circular towers, which afterwards were enclosed in polygonal masonry. Between the two southerly towers there was a vaulted gateway, which much later was decorated with frescoes in a Byzantine style, though the Latin inscriptions and armorial details show that they were commissioned by Franks. The most probable date is the end of the thirteenth century. This very unusual monument, which can be seen at the discretion of the officials of the Museum, was walled in by the

Venetians after the Turkish attack of 1463, when they banked up this section of the wall and moved the entrance to its present position at the south corner. The Toron Castle in front, within which the Xenia Hotel has been built, is a Venetian structure of about 1400, designed as a forward protection of the entrance, and a wet ditch was dug from the north shore as far as the later Grimani bastion. The fortification of the island of Bourtzi at the entrance to the harbour followed in 1471, though this was modernised later. Conscientiously restored as a hotel and restaurant, it gives a good impression of the new type of military architecture that developed when cannons had come into use. Further defences were constructed by the Venetians in the early eighteenth century, notably the entrance on the north side of the Castle of the Greeks, three bastions defending the harbour and land approach (of which there survives only the Grimani bastion in front of the Toron Castle) and of course the fortress of Palamidhi.

Palamidhi was connected to Acronauplia by a protected stairway of—it is said—857 steps, or one can make the ascent by car, turning right at the cross-roads on the outskirts of the town and then left and after that winding up to the gate. The defences, built in 1711–14, consist of seven artillery forts and a curtain wall, to which the Turks added a bastion at the southern end. Palamidhi, which has no natural supply of water, was not intended to be a place of habitation, but simply an enormous outwork for the defence of the citadel and town below, much as Toron Castle had been three hundred years earlier when artillery had a shorter range. Its preservation is excellent and the visitor can appreciate for himself the principles of these highly scientific fortifications.

The Museum, at the end of Syntagma Square, is a handsome Venetian building of about 1713, designed for barracks in spite of the inscription, which was inserted recently. It contains the finds from ancient Asine and the sites near Dendra (or Midea) and Berbati as well as some of the less showy material from Tiryns and Mycenae. Though its main importance is for students of Mycenaean pottery, the exhibits are set out attractively and there are for less specialised visitors the remains of Mycenaean armour from a tholos tomb near Dendra and a group of grotesque terracotta masks from Tiryns, made not much later than 700 B.C. and presumably intended as dedications in a sanctuary.

In the town the only medieval building is the church of St Sophia, a simple nave with an apse at the east and a dome in the middle. The window in the apse is a sort of Gothic, perhaps around 1400, but the main building might be older. Much more distinguished is the conventual

9

church of Ayia Moni in the district of Aria. The way to it is by the road to Epidaurus, turning off right after a mile and following for another mile a roughish track up to the convent, set inconspicuously into the slope of the hillside. This slope disturbs the proportions of the church, which generally resembles that of Merbaka, but is rather severer in its exterior decoration and has an exonarthex; the marble crosses in the walls recall Chonika; and again the belfry is a later addition. The interior gives some idea of the original effect, though the paintings and the screen are replacements. Documents and an inscription on the west facade date this church between 1143 and 1149; the other conventual buildings are fairly modern, but keep to the traditional plan and give a good impression of the coenobitic rule, anyhow for females. For the monks of the Orthodox Church the ideal life is one of contemplation, but nuns are expected to be more industrious and at Ayia Moni they weave on hand looms with a skill that is professional and not merely folklorish. On ordinary days there is no danger of missing a visit to the workroom and shop.

Asine

The deserted site of ancient Asine is about 7 miles by road from Nauplia. One starts on the highway to Epidaurus, after $2\frac{1}{2}$ miles branches off right for Tolo and, keeping right after 2 miles, passes through the village of modern Asine (formerly Tseferagha). Beyond it the road forks left for ancient Asine and right for Tolo, and the two places are also connected by a road along the shore. The site is on a small steep promontory with remains of fortifications and at the west, where access is easiest, a little white church. Excavation, carried out by the Swedes, has shown that this Asine was inhabited through the Bronze and Early Iron Ages, was destroyed (by Argos) just before 700 B.C., revived and was fortified in the Hellenistic period, and became part of a country estate under the Romans. In the Second World War it received an Italian garrison. Round the hill there are some good stretches of the Hellenistic wall, near the church remains of a Roman bath building and some houses of the Middle Bronze Age, and at the summit inscriptions of imperial Italy; the other ruins provide an exercise in dating. A visit to Asine is recommended particularly to bathers, since the shore is sandy and at Tolo, which welcomes campers, there is almost a plage.

Epidaurus   (*Fig.* 19)

For tourists and archaeologists Epidaurus usually means the Sanctuary
of Asklepios. The ancient city to which it belonged, now called Palea
Epidhavros (or Old Epidaurus), was 5 miles away in a direct line and
much further by road. At present the usual way to the sanctuary is by
the road from Nauplia, going straight over the crossing near the edge
of the town and after 17 miles forking right in Ligurio to reach the site
in another 2½ miles; the left fork at Ligurio leads to Old Epidaurus. Soon
there should also be a highway running directly from Corinth to the
sanctuary, and this will both shorten the journey from Athens and alter
the regular pattern of tours round the Argolid.

Along the road from Nauplia to the sanctuary there are some interesting antiquities for the visitor who is not hurried. After 9 miles, near
kilometre stone 14 and just before a deep ravine, an ancient bridge
crosses a gully on the left of the road. It is constructed of huge blocks of
stone, like those of the citadel walls of Mycenae and Tiryns, but may
be much later. This style of masonry is often called Cyclopean, a name
that goes back at least to the fifth century B.C., when legend had attributed it to the Cyclopes, the race of one-eyed giants who gave trouble to
Odysseus; but though it can be considered characteristically Mycenaean, the technique is more cumbersome than difficult and recurs
occasionally in later times. About half a mile beyond the bridge and
again on the left the ruins of a fortress can be seen on a hill. This was a
post on the frontier between Epidaurus and Argos, and goes back
probably to the Classical period. Further on, at the far end of Ligurio
village, the church of St John stands on the right of the road. Stylis-
tically it is fairly close to Chonika, for example in the patterns of the
brickwork, but it is smaller and relatively shorter, since at the east the
dome is supported not on columns but on the piers of the sanctuary.
It is thought to be of the end of the eleventh century.

The sanctuary of Epidaurus lies at the foot of a hill, surrounded by
the welcome shade of pine trees and watered by mildly alkaline springs.
Its patron Asklepios, a late recruit to the divine family, was a healing
god of professional status, whose cult spread suddenly over Greece at
the end of the fifth century B.C. The earliest finds from the site are no
earlier than the sixth century and it seems that at Epidaurus (as at
Corinth) Asklepios took over from Apollo; anyhow patients who came to
consult Asklepios had first to sacrifice to Apollo Maleatas and the
sanctuary of this Apollo—to judge from the finds—was older than that

of Asklepios. By the early fourth century B.C. Asklepios was drawing
enough Greeks from other states to justify the enlargement of the four-
yearly games and an extensive programme of building, and he was as
popular as ever in Roman times. Even when Paganism was made
illegal in the late fourth century A.D. the Christian authorities thought it
advisable to put up a largish church in this remote place, perhaps to
continue the miraculous cures under more sanctified management, but

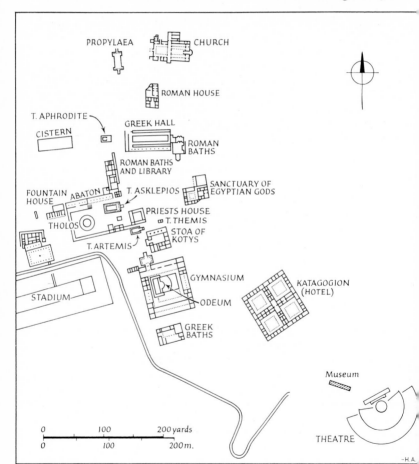

Fig. 19. Epidaurus, Sanctuary of Asklepios.

if so the Slav invasions swept away even the memory of the medical properties of the Asklepieion. The site was excavated by the Greeks about the end of the last century. Visitors in the summer should find out the dates of the modern Festival, so that they can attend or avoid it; the programme consists of ancient dramas produced in the modern fashion to the satisfaction, artistic or social, of thousands of Athenians and foreigners.

The Theatre, which is near the pay gate, was one of the finest of Greek theatres and luckily has not suffered much alteration or damage. The gateways were added probably around 300 B.C., the stage was remodelled at the same time but has collapsed, and recently the end walls of the auditorium have been rebuilt and the seats tidied up. Yet even so the visitor has a remarkably pure impression of a standard theatre of the fourth century B.C. The orchestra is circular and, since it was there that most of the action or at least the movement took place, there was no reason other than convenience of siting why the auditorium should not go more than halfway round it, though it is less obvious why the curve of the seats avoids strict circularity and is based on three centres. The stage, beyond and a little wider than the orchestra, was a separate structure; the platform, eventually about 11 feet high and faced with Ionic half-columns, was reached by a ramp on each side and had as its back wall a building one storey higher. The acoustics are excellent, but one should remember when watching the guides' tricks that the middle of the orchestra was occupied by an altar. According to Pausanias the architect of the Theatre was a Polyclitus of Argos who built the Tholos too, and this would date the Theatre about the middle of the fourth century B.C.; another theory, more ingenious than probable, is that there were two stages of construction, both Hellenistic. The capacity has been reckoned as 14,000, though such figures are not precisely reliable; first we do not know how much space should be allowed for each person, and secondly—a point of importance when comparing the sizes of theatres—the modern estimates are not all based on the same allowance. It is a pity that the seats were not numbered, though probably this would have been as useless a precaution as often in modern Greece.

Many tourists spend half an hour listening, photographing and being photographed in the Theatre, perhaps take a look at the Museum, and then drive back to Nauplia, but there is more to see in the sanctuary. Going down from the Theatre one comes first to the Katagogion or Hotel, a two-storeyed square block with 160 rooms round four colonnaded inner courts. As in many Greek buildings the walls were of plastered mud brick (which has disappeared) on a stone base. There are Roman repairs and alterations in the north-eastern half. To the west are the ruins of Greek Baths and a Greek Gymnasium (or perhaps rather Palaestra) with a Roman Odeum (or roofed theatre) built inside it. Typically the Greek remains are of squared stone without mortar, the Roman of fired brick set in mortar—a distinction that is very important for survival, since squared stone invites re-use but brick-work does not. Opposite the Gymnasium's elaborate porch was a small Temple of Artemis and beyond it a much altered block known as the Priests' House, but originally perhaps a hall where patients slept before the big stoa was built in the fourth century B.C.

The platform of the Temple of Asklepios is worth noticing because of the reconstruction of its upper parts in the Museum and the records of its building, which were inscribed on a marble slab and have survived nearly complete. From these we learn that the total cost was between 23 and 24 talents or the equivalent of 140,000 days wages for a skilled craftsman. Much of the cost went on the quarrying and transport (by ox-cart and ship) of limestone from Corinth and marble from Attica. The building committee let out various jobs or parts of jobs to private individuals and deducted fines, some of as much as fifty per cent, for lateness on fulfilment of contracts. The work—of decoration as well as construction—was completed in four years and eight months, though we are not told which those years were. Still, style and names show that the temple must have been built in the first half of the fourth century B.C.

Behind the Temple is the Tholos, the architect of which is said to have been the same Polyclitus who constructed the Theatre. It was a lavish circular building, as can be judged from the reconstructions in the Museum, and cost 50 talents or rather more than twice as much as the Temple, partly because of its material (since marble took five times as long to work as limestone). The concentric foundations correspond to the colonnades and wall, but the basement doorways and their disposition defy rational explanation. On the north there stretched the Abaton, a long stoa which had a lower storey at the west where the ground fell. This was where patients spent the night, hoping for Asklepios to heal or advise them in a dream, and sometimes put up inscriptions testifying to his success or to that of the treatment prescribed by the priests. At the east end of the stoa the Roman baths and library of Antoninus (not the emperor) overlie a structure probably of the fifth century B.C. To the north-east there were a large Greek hall and another Roman set of baths. In the central area, which reached from these baths to beyond the Tholos and was fortified in the third or fourth century A.D., several semi-circular marble benches stand around; they go by the name of 'exedras' and are common dedications in sanctuaries. The ruins of the Propylaea, across the ancient road from the city of Epidaurus, are near the north end of the archaeological precinct; its columns were Ionic outside and Corinthian within. To the east one can make out the plan of a basilical church with doubled aisles and a large forecourt; it is probably of the fifth century A.D. More or less contemporary but not so intelligible are the remains of a big Roman house, which stood halfway between the church and the Greek hall. The Stadium, outside the modern perimeter, is pleasantly sited in what was once a natural hollow. Its plan is rect-angular, starting lines survive at each end, and a vaulted tunnel runs under the present road to a large complex with a colonnaded court. The Greeks understood the principles of the arch, but usually till Roman times did not care to use it above ground; the reason must have been aesthetic.

Most of the Greek buildings are of the fourth or early third century B.C. and the Roman of the second century A.D., but the Priests' House may go back to the mid sixth century B.C., as perhaps does the sacred well at the east end of the Abaton. There are probably other early structures under those of the fourth century, but in general the excava-tors did not probe below them. Still the loss of archaeological know-ledge is compensated by the tidiness and homogeneity of the site.

The Museum, near the Theatre, is too narrow for proper display and circulation. The first room contains statues of Roman date, inscriptions testifying to cures, two inscriptions with the accounts for the building of the Temple of Asklepois and the Tholos, and (in a case) some ancient surgical instruments. In the other rooms, besides architectural pieces and more Roman statues, there are useful reconstructions of the various parts of the Tholos which are worth the thinking needed to understand them, a reconstruction of part of the Temple of Asklepios, and casts and a few original bits of its elegant sculpture, but the best and most com-plete figures are in the National Museum at Athens. For an appreciation of Classical architecture this is the most helpful museum in Greece.

At the top of the hill above the theatre what is left of the sanctuary of Apollo Maleatas has been uncovered. The path now starts beyond the theatre and leads up behind it, but it is as well to ask one of the guards for directions. The climb takes officially 15 minutes. Here there was a settlement during the Bronze Age and perhaps a cult place, to judge by the finds of Mycenaean 'idols' (very simplified female figurines of terracotta). In the seventh century B.C. an altar was set up; in the fourth century B.C. a little temple, a stoa and a cistern were added; and in the second century A.D. Antoninus completed the ensemble with a fountain and a house for the priest. The view is more impressive than the ruins.

Argos   (*Plate* 10, *Fig.* 20)

Argos is a dusty town, too busy for tourism and the past, but it has a fair share of antiquities. It lies about 4 miles from the sea below two hills, the high conical Larissa and the low dome of the Aspis (or Shield).

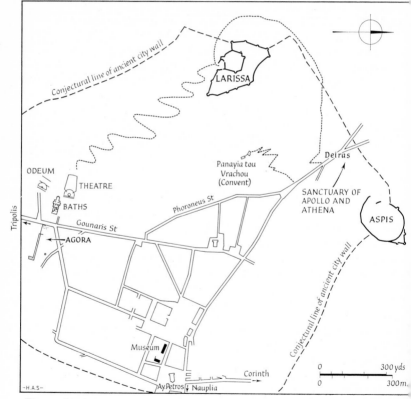

Fig. 20. Argos.

Plate 10. Argos from Nauplia (telephoto). The Larissa is in the centre, the Aspis at the right just beyond the modern town.

Settlement began at latest in the Middle Bronze Age; in the Mycenaean period legends, its situation and a wall on the Larissa suggest that the site must have been important; graves prove occupation throughout the Early Iron Age; in the Archaic and Classical periods Argos competed unsuccessfully with Sparta for dominance in the Peloponnese, but succeeded in conquering the other cities round the Argive plain; in later antiquity it remained prosperous if politically second rate; and in spite of damage by the barbarian raids of A.D. 267 and 395 survived the Middle Ages. Continuous inhabitation and a thorough destruction by Ibrahim Pasha in 1825 have razed or buried most of the remains of earlier Argos and except on the outskirts of the modern town large scale excavation is impracticable, but the Museum and the melons can be recommended.

Most of the excavation has been done by the French (with the Dutch).

The main area is at the south, straddling the road to Tripolis where it turns half-left. On the east side, where part of the ancient Agora has been cleared, vestiges can be seen of a hall with internal columns, built in the fifth century B.C., and beyond it of a long colonnade of much the same date; after the disaster of A.D. 395 the hall was replaced by a smaller edifice and the stoa remodelled. The circular remains further on belong to a Roman nymphaeum (an ornamental pavilion with flowing water). Across the road the ruins of the Roman baths are unusually well preserved and intelligible. The apsidal part of the west end was a sort of memorial hall, next came the dressing room, then the cold plunge, and at the east one principal and two lesser hot baths. The arrangements for heating are clear enough. This establishment goes back to the second century A.D., but was repaired and altered in the fourth. The theatre, beyond the baths, has lost both sides of its auditorium but is said to have held 20,000 spectators. It was built around 300 B.C. and remodelled in the second and fourth centuries A.D. The visitor who has been to Epidaurus and Athens should be able to sort out the periods. South of the theatre was a roofed odeum of Roman date; it was put up over the earlier meeting place of the Argive assembly, from which there survive the straight rows of seats at the back.

Near-by a path leads up in about three quarters of an hour to the citadel on the Larissa. It consists of an inner and an outer enclosure, and at least since Classical times the inner fortifications have followed the same lines. Here stretches of the Greek wall are visible in various styles, at one place still 30 feet high, but the rest of the curtains are hard to date. Some may be Byzantine, since in the early thirteenth century the defences of Argos were in good enough repair to hold out against the Franks for seven years. These new occupants constructed some good towers on the Larissa and later the Turks added the outer enclosure and emplacements for artillery, but the Venetians in their tenures from 1394 to 1463 and again from 1686 to 1715 concentrated on Nauplia and did little or nothing to improve Argos. The inner enclosure has suffered inside from old-fashioned archaeological zeal, which stripped out most of the medieval remains in a search for ancient foundations or relics and dumped the spoil untidily outside. The castle on the Larissa is worth a visit, but so are many other castles in Greece.

From the hilltop one can follow the probable line of the city wall of the third century B.C.—down the south ridge and past the odeum, then swinging round beyond the further square in the modern town and up the east side of the Aspis (with another acropolis), and from there

returning to the citadel on the Larissa. One can also view the excavations at Deiras, at the foot of the Aspis just east of the road between the
two hills. Here there was an ancient sanctuary of Apollo and Athena,
in which churches were built in the fifth century and the Middle Byzantine period, but it is a messy site.

The Museum, on the west of the principal square of the town, is a
spacious and well arranged building, which contains finds from Argos
and Lerna. The main rooms have a good show of pottery of the Bronze
and Early Iron Ages, the earliest suit of hoplite—that is heavy infantry
—armour yet discovered (of about 700 B.C.), and long iron spits of a
type that were serving as currency in the Peloponnese in the seventh
century B.C. In an annexe there is upstairs a collection of statuary of
Roman date, much of it found in the baths, and some curiously clumsy
grave reliefs, carved in a flaky local stone; but so far there is nothing
from the great Classical masters of Argos, of whom Polyclitus (of an
earlier generation than the architect who worked at Epidaurus) was
classed with Phidias. Below, a room is devoted to the finds from Lerna.
All this is humdrum or specialised material, though it is worth glancing
at the exuberant wildness of the later Argive Geometric pottery, if only
to appreciate the ironwork of the Museum doors. Outside and to the
right, under a modern stoa in the courtyard, there are some excellent
mosaics of the fifth century A.D., including a complete set of the months
of the year, found in a house not far from the theatre.

Lerna

Just beyond the village of Mili, about 6 miles south of Argos on the
road to Tripolis, a large shed on the left marks the site of Lerna, recently
excavated by the Americans with results of surprising significance for
Greek prehistory. Here the mound left by a Neolithic settlement was
levelled for new building in the second phase of the Early Bronze Age
and fortified with a double wall and towers. Later the ordinary houses
were cleared away for a large rectangular structure roofed with terracotta tiles, to which the round building at Tiryns is for importance the
only parallel yet known from Greece of that time. This 'House of the
Tiles' was burnt down about 2200 B.C., perhaps in an invasion which
destroyed other settlements in the Argolid and Attica. In the last phase
of the Early Bronze Age the mound formed by its debris was at first left
vacant, though houses were built round it, and a modest and unfortified
village continued to use the site till the end of the Bronze Age.

The excavators have left exposed houses of the Neolithic period and the Early and Middle Bronze Ages. These houses, of course, were not all standing at the same time. The House of the Tiles, protected by a shed, is more impressive and the method of construction—plastered mud-brick on a stone footing—is plain to see. The two areas floored with pebbles are the bottoms of Mycenaean shaft graves, which were sunk into the mound much later. There are also intelligible remains of the fortifications. The tiles protecting some mud brick walls and the patches of cement are of course modern, but some of the ancient tiles are piled in a corner of the shed. The finds are in the Museum of Argos.

As might be expected, there are ruins of another Frankish castle on the hill above Lerna.

7 · Arcadia

Arcadia, in the middle of the Peloponnese, is a country of pleasant landscapes with rolling upland and forests as well as mountains. Its centre now is Tripolis, which is connected by good roads with Argos, Sparta, Megalopolis and Messenia, and (by way of Vlacherna and Langadhia) Olympia. Another road to Olympia, much of it rough, goes from Megalopolis through Andritsena, from which a side road leads to Bassae. Tripolis has several good hotels and Andritsena one.

In ancient times Arcadia was a backward region, and it was only in the fourth century B.C. that the Theban leader Epaminondas established a moderately effective confederation of its scattered communities, not from a love of progress but to keep Sparta in check. Even so, Arcadia has never had an important place in Greek history except as a supplier of mercenary soldiers and its fame comes from the idyllic fantasy of its pastoral life, invented by Hellenistic poets who lived in the big cities overseas.

Tripolis, originally an Albanian settlement, was founded in the fourteenth century A.D. and destroyed completely by Ibrahim in 1828 in reprisal for the massacre of its Turkish inhabitants a few years earlier. Some time perhaps it will be excavated for information about the late Medieval and Turkish periods of Greece; meanwhile visitors who miss archaeological remains can console themselves with good Greek cooking.

Tegea

The plain of Tripolis was divided in antiquity between Mantinea in the north and Tegea in the south. These were politically the most advanced of the Arcadian communities and had become urbanised before Epaminondas. There is not much to see of Mantinea except the base of the city wall, and at Tegea the only considerable remains belong to the temple of Athena Alea. To reach them one takes the road from Tripolis to Sparta, turns left after 5 miles at Kerasitsa onto a side road sign-posted 'Archaia Tegea' (though the village is more often called Piali), and in a mile or so finds another signpost to the Museum and the Temple. The temple, excavated by the French, was built in the mid fourth century B.C. with foundations of conglomerate and superstructure of a local marble that has weathered a darkish grey. The plan is clear and there are enough Doric members tumbled around to show what the elevation was. The effect is agreeably melancholy. The Museum contains minor fragments of the sculpture of the temple and casts of the better pieces (which are in the National Museum in Athens) as well as fine specimens of its architectural mouldings. Of the remaining sculpture much is of Roman date, though more entertaining than usual. There are also some interesting small bronzes of late Geometric and Archaic styles both from the sanctuary of Athena Alea and from a sanctuary of Athena and Posidon at Asea (about 10 miles away in the direction of Megalopolis), and also a selection of pottery—from the Neolithic to the Middle Bronze periods—found at Ayioryitika about 7 miles east of Tripolis.

Megalopolis   (*Fig.* 21)

The ruins of ancient Megalopolis lie about half a mile from the modern town, along the road to Andritsena. It was founded in 371 B.C. by the Theban general Epaminondas to be the capital of the new Arcadian confederacy, which he had created as a counterweight to Sparta. The city was laid out on the grand scale, with a wall about 5 miles in circumference, and peopled by drafts from older Arcadian communities, but (like the modern town) did not fulfil its planners' hopes and in the second century A.D. was largely in ruins. The site was excavated by the British.

Just before the bridge a track leads to the theatre, set into a steep slope and now overshadowed by a wood. It is thought that it was built in the late fourth century B.C. and improved with a stone stage a hundred years later. Its capacity was very large, perhaps about 20,000. In front of it was the Thersilion, so named after its donor, which was built around 370 B.C. for the meetings of the 10,000 members of the federal assembly. It was a rectangular covered hall and, since Greek methods of building did not allow wide spans, the roof was supported by rows of pillars set radially to the speaker's platform which was a little forward of centre. In this way the audience's view was much less obstructed than in the earlier Telesterion at Eleusis. It seems also that the floor of the auditorium sloped or was tiered down to the platform. A deep portico stood out at the front of the hall and when the theatre was first built served as

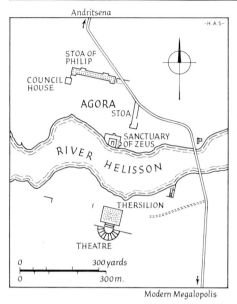

Andritsena

-H.A.S-

STOA OF
PHILIP

COUNCIL
HOUSE

AGORA
STOA

SANCTUARY
OF ZEUS

RIVER HELISSON

THERSILION

THEATRE

0   300 yards

0   300 m.

Fig. 21.
Megalopolis.

Modern Megalopolis

a background for its very low stage. Only some foundations of the
Thersilion are still in place. Scattered about in the fields on both sides
of the river other ruins can be discerned, but they are easier to follow
on a plan.

Bassae

The temple of Bassae is 9 miles from Andritsena up a good road.
Andritsena, which still keeps the appearance of an old-fashioned hill
town and has a remarkable library in its school, is 21 miles from
Megalopolis by a rough road and 27 miles from the coastal highway below
Krestena by a road equally rough in its first lap. Apart from Bassae the
only place of archaeological note along these routes is Karytena, halfway
between Megalopolis and Andritsena.

Karytena has a castle, built by the Franks in 1254, acquired by the
Byzantines in 1320, seized by the Turks around 1460, and occupied by
the Greeks in the War of Independence. The lower parts of the walls
are Frankish, as presumably is the rather Italianate hall. In themselves
the ruins of this castle are not of much interest, but their situation on a

hill that rises sheer from the river Alpheus makes one of the most romantic views in Greece.

Bassae stands high up on a mountainside to the south of Andritsena. The sanctuary belonged to the city of Phigalia, the most westerly community of Arcadia, about 2½ hours away on foot, and according to Pausanias the existing temple was built by Ictinus, the architect of the Parthenon, as a thank-offering of the Phigalians to Apollo for delivering them from a plague in the 420's. All Pausanias's statements are disputed and some students put the building a little earlier. Some time after the second century A.D. the temple was damaged by earthquake, but the place was remote and the ruins were left untouched. So at the beginning of this century the Greeks were able to do a creditable restoration of the cella walls, though some of the floor blocks were put back the wrong way round, and fragments of the coffered ceiling still lie around the site. The temple was built in the Doric style (*Plate* 4) of a fine but brittle local limestone, is unexpectedly narrow in plan, faces north, and has a side door in the east wall of the cella. In the interior of the cella spur walls project from the sides and terminate in Ionic half-columns, and the free standing column at the end (as perhaps its two neighbours) had a Corinthian capital—the first known example in Greek architecture. Above these columns there was a sculptured frieze, found in 1811–12 by the German and British philhellenes who removed the pedimental sculptures from Aegina, but this time sold to the British Museum. The temple is impressive for its relative completeness, its quality and its situation, and on a clear day the view from the site is excellent, though since Bassae is over 3,700 feet above sea level it is sometimes in the clouds.

Lycosura   (*Fig.* 22)

About 2 miles from Megalopolis on the main road to Kalamata and just beyond the bridge over the Alpheus a roughish track leads off on the right, signposted to Archaia Lykosoura among other places. After a mile or so one forks right, again at a signpost, and passes on through oak woods till almost exactly 5 miles from the main road the lonely Museum of Lycosura can be seen on the ridge on the left. Though a short side track goes up to the Museum, it is better to walk from here than to drive.

Lycosura was a small Arcadian community, which Pausanias (unconfirmed by archaeologists) called the oldest of all cities. It possessed

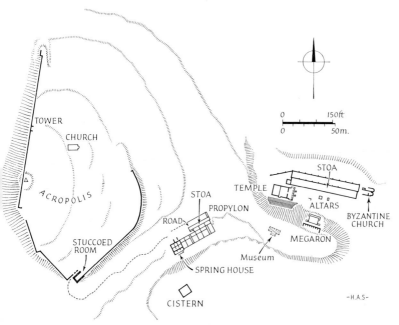

Fig. 22. Lycosura. *By courtesy of E. Vanderpool.*

a sanctuary of Despoina (or Mistress), who was equated with Persephone. This sanctuary lies below the Museum on a shelf on the hillside. The temple, in the Doric style, was prostyle—that is, it had a colonnade at the front only. This colonnade was of marble, but the cella behind had walls of mud brick on a limestone base, in part preserved to its full height. As at Bassae, there was a side door to the cella. Close to the temple on the south is a row of steps, presumably a retaining wall and not a place for watching some mysterious spectacle. East of the steps are the ruins of a platform with a court in front, which Pausanias called the 'megaron' though they may have belonged to a big altar. Opposite are traces of three altars and a stoa. The temple is probably of the early second century B.C. and the other structures should be of much the same date. On the other side of the Museum there are more ruins, of which the clearest are those of a fountain house and a cistern, both probably Hellenistic. On the hilltop just above there are some ancient and medieval remains of the walls of the acropolis.

10

The Museum was built because transport of the finds was difficult at the time of the main excavation (which was done by the Greeks) and indeed the present track was not built till the 1960's. The principal exhibit is the residue of the group of colossal marble statues carved by Damophon in the second century B.C. or second A.D. and set up across the width of the west end of the temple. There were four of these figures —Demeter and Despoina seated in the centre with Artemis and the obscure Anytos standing at the sides. The heads are casts from the originals, which are now in Athens. There are also mediocre fragments of other sculptures, pieces of temple furniture, and inscriptions which show that in Roman times the sanctuary was still patronised by wealthy Megapolitans.

The track goes on for 6 miles or so from Lycosura to Karyes below Mt Lykaion, and from Karyes it is half an hour's walk to the remains of the hippodrome, where chariot races were held. Beside it there are the ruins of a stoa, a hostel and fountain houses, all probably Hellenistic. The peak, about 15 minutes south-west, has the remains of an altar of Zeus and another excellent view.

8 · Laconia

Laconia is the south-east part of the Peloponnese. The main road crosses the hills from Tripolis to Sparta, which lies in the sheltered valley of the Eurotas between the towering range of Taygetus and the lower mass of Parnon. From Sparta the road runs on to the port of Yithion (Gytheum) and about half-way a branch leads off eastwards to Monemvasia. A rough road over Taygetus sometimes connects Sparta directly with Kalamata, and another road—in part roughish—leads round from Yithion through Areopolis to Kalamata; but by car it is often as quick and always more comfortable to go round by Tripolis. There are good hotels at Sparta and one at Monemvasia.

The prehistory of Laconia is obscure, though it was important in the Mycenaean period, if one may judge from the legend of Menelaus's kingdom and the rich finds in the tholos tomb at Vaphio, 4 miles south of modern Sparta. In the Early Iron Age the Spartans of history appear. They were or became a small ruling group, which had subjected or enslaved the other inhabitants of Laconia and in the later eighth century did the same by Messenia. To maintain their position the Spartans militarised their society, starting barrack life at the age of seven and making themselves the best trained and disciplined infantry in the Greek world. So in the sixth century they were able to dominate the Peloponnese and became the leading Greek state, in the fifth they were challenged by the new naval imperialism of Athens, and in the fourth they emerged supreme to be defeated disastrously by Thebes in 371. After this Sparta, now limited to Laconia, was a minor though dangerous power and in the second century even their Laconian subjects became independent. Under Roman rule Laconia was moderately prosperous till the Barbarian invasions, and from the seventh century onwards the Slav tribes who had occupied Taygetus were a constant menace. The Franks came about 1205, the Byzantines returned in 1262, and the Turks followed in 1460, though Venice held Monemvasia till 1540 and had a short suzerainty from 1686 to 1715.

Sparta   (*Fig.* 23)

Sparta seems first to have become important in the Early Iron Age, but it was not until the Hellenistic period that it was defended by a city wall. In early Roman times it received a new magnificence, and though plundered by the Goths and Herulians in A.D. 267 and burnt by Alaric in 395, it survived well down the Middle Ages under the new name of Lacedaemonia. In 1262 its inhabitants abandoned the old site for the security of Mistra, now garrisoned by the Byzantines, nor did they return till 1834, when modern Sparta was laid out by the king of Bavaria to become (he hoped) the peer of the new Athens, though till very recently it looked more like a ghost town.

The visible remains of ancient Sparta are disappointing. A track on the left side of the football ground, north of the town, leads in not much more than $\frac{1}{4}$ mile to the pleasantly wooded hillock of the acropolis. Here there can be seen the foundations of the church and mortuary chapel of Holy Nikon, who converted Slavs; the church, though basilical in plan is of the tenth century, and the chapel a little later. To the north-west, near the water tower, a length of foundation has been exposed of the temple of Athena Chalkioikos built in the sixth century B.C., and south-west of that is the theatre, probably constructed in the late first century B.C. though the stage (which goes back earlier) was remodelled on and off till the fourth century A.D. The wall round the acropolis is partly of the third and fourth centuries A.D. and partly later, while the slit trenches at the north edge date from the recent civil war. The so-called 'Tomb of Leonidas', a couple of hundred yards west of the football ground, was a small temple perhaps of the third century B.C. The celebrated sanctuary of Artemis Orthia is near the river, down a lane to the right at the first bend of the road to Tripolis after it leaves the town. Here there are the foundations of a small temple built towards the middle of the sixth century B.C. above the foundations of a smaller temple and itself rebuilt in the Hellenistic period. In front stood an altar, where Spartan girls sang and—anyhow in Roman times, when a sentimental antiquarianism was cultivated—boys were beaten to show their toughness. The little theatre round the altar was built in the third century A.D. for the comfort of the spectators. Though a comic little site, the finds made here were important for archaeology.

The Museum, stocked largely by the British excavations, is worth a visit. In the entrance hall there are curious reliefs of Roman date with inset iron sickles, awarded to boys as prizes in competitions. The first

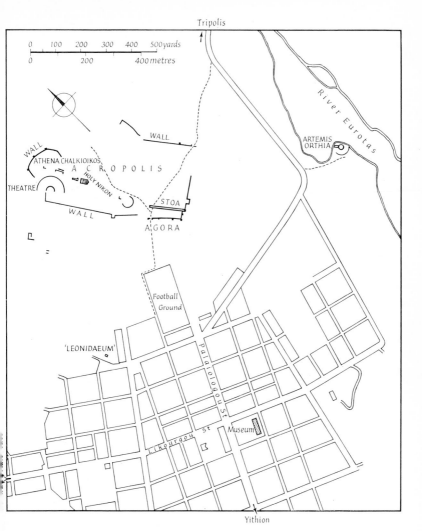

Fig. 23. Sparta.

two rooms on the right contain grave reliefs with the typical Spartan
subjects of the seated hero and votive reliefs showing Castor and Pollux
(the Dioscuri); these date from the sixth century B.C. onwards. The third
room has miscellaneous sculpture (mostly notably the upper part of a
soldier—the so-called 'Leonidas'—of the 470's B.C.), some interesting

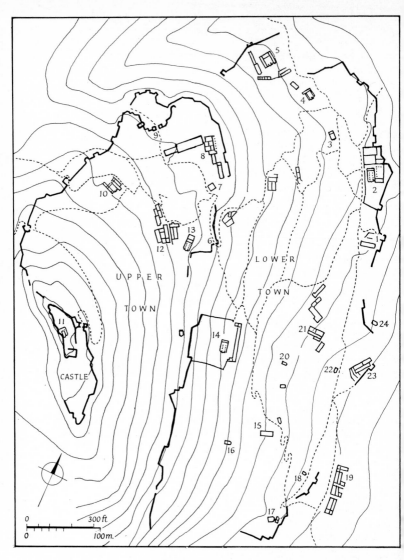

Fig. 24. **Mistra.** Contours are notional. 1, gate. 2, Metropolis. 3, Evangelistria. 4, Sts Theodore. 5, Afendiko. 6, Monemvasia Gate. 7, mosque. 8, Palace. 9, Nauplia Gate. 10, Ay. Sophia. 11, chapels. 12, 'Little Palace'. 13, St Nicholas. 14, Pantanassa. 15, 'Frangopoulos' house. 16, Ay. Taxiarchai. 17, Peribleptos. 18, St George. 19, Krevatas house. 20, St Anne. 21, 'Lascaris' house. 22, St Christopher. 23, Marmara fountain. 24, St John.

Plate 11.
Air view of Mistra from the north-east. The Metropolis is centre bottom, the Palace near the top on the right, the wall surrounding Pantanassa opposite at the left edge.

architectural pieces from the 'Throne of Apollo' at Amyclae (an elaborate altar with mixed Doric and Ionic members of the later sixth century B.C.), inscriptions, Mycenaean weapons and pottery from various parts of Laconia, and other small objects. On the left of the entrance the first room illustrates well the lively parochialism of Archaic Spartan art in painted pottery, ivory seals, cut-out little figures of lead, bronze statuettes and grotesque masks of terracotta. The next room has Roman sculpture and there is more in the garden. Some well preserved if mediocre mosaics of about the third century A.D. have been left where they were found in the modern town; if one wishes to see them, it is best to ask at the Museum.

Mistra   (*Fig.* 24, *Plate* 11)

Mistra is 3 miles west of Sparta on a very steep hill on the fringe of Taygetus. The site was not occupied till A.D. 1249, when the Franks built a castle on the top to check Slav raiders. Thirteen years later in part payment of a ransom this castle was handed over to the Byzantine emperor, who made Mistra a base from which to recover and govern the Peloponnese, and as the empire dwindled elsewhere the city which had sprung up under the protection of the castle became of almost metropolitan importance. In 1460 Mistra surrendered to the Turks, but continued to prosper and at the arrival of the Venetians in 1687 had a population of 42,000 and a busy trade in silk. After the Turks returned in 1715 it continued to be the second largest place in the Peloponnese until in 1770 the Russians incited a revolt of the Maniates of the south of Taygetus and Mistra was first looted by Greeks and then burnt by Turks. The destruction was completed by Ibrahim Pasha in 1825 and the site deserted, though the castle came into use again in the civil war of 1943–9.

The city below the castle was in two parts, both fortified, and there were suburbs outside the walls. It is thought that the wall of the upper town was built very soon after 1262 and the lower circuit at the beginning of the next century. The division between the two towns follows the contour below the Palace and above Pantanassa, but now appears as little more than a terrace wall. Under the Byzantines the upper town was the aristocratic quarter with the Palace, its church of Ayia Sophia and the houses of notables and dependants of the court, while the lower town had the Metropolis (or cathedral), several monasteries and of course more houses. In both the city and the suburbs there were also many little chapels and a few fountains. Altogether the remains of more than 2,000 buildings have been counted, mostly ruined in the late eighteenth or early nineteenth century and offering a vast field to Byzantinists. So far it is the churches that have had most attention, and since the 1890's they and some of the chapels have been more or less thoroughly restored. At the same time their paintings, which were suffering badly from exposure to the weather, have been cleaned or uncovered and repaired. Some work has been done on the Palace too, and perhaps it will soon be the turn of the houses, which range in date from the mid thirteenth to the early nineteenth centuries.

For most visitors the principal attractions of Mistra are the paintings and architecture of its Late Byzantine churches. In both arts there is a tendency to picturesque incoherence, but the paintings have a livelier or at least more animated originality and with their warmer expression of humanity they seem to be straining, if erratically, towards a new style. Variation on the old is more the effect of the ecclesiastical architecture of Mistra, which absorbed a few characteristics from Italy (presumably through the Franks) but, unlike the Serbian and Bulgarian provinces of Orthodox Christianity, did not develop radically new species of churches. The Middle Byzantine types continue, though usually elongated and masked by annexes, and there is a novel fusion of the cross in square with the basilical plan; exteriors are often enriched with ornamental brickwork, but the masonry is not so neat; and inside the painting takes less account than before of the architectural space. In general decorative effect is more important than clarity of design, certainly when judged by Middle Byzantine standards; for proof of this one needs only to look down at the roofs of the Metropolis or Pantanassa. The chapels are more sober in form, since they usually consist of a single barrel-vaulted nave and, even if the decoration is elaborate, it is not so obtrusive.

Mistra is a place of which most visitors keep only confused memories, since they try to see too much in a single comprehensive tour. It is wiser to select a few monuments and resolutely ignore the others, or to spend parts of two (or more) days there, starting early in the morning before the coach parties come from Tripolis. The ruins of a deserted town benefit from solitude and the churches are too small to share with a crowd.

The best entrance to the site is through the gateway a little before the Xenia cafe and near the Metropolis. This was the cathedral church, dedicated to St Demetrius, and had a bishop's palace attached. The church, which has had some recent restoration, was laid out in the early fourteenth century on a basilical plan, but its upper storey was replaced at the beginning of the fifteenth by one of cross in square plan and orna- ter style. The exonarthex, belfry and north portico are also additions to the original church. The carving inside is of various dates; the leaf capitals are very early Byzantine (except for the two modern substitutes at the east), the iconostasis (or screen) is a recently restored amalgam of Middle and Late Byzantine pieces, and the bishop's throne is a good specimen of seventeenth century woodwork. In the middle of the floor the slab with a double-headed eagle is said without much evidence to commemorate the coronation there in 1449 of the last of the Byzantine emperors. The paintings, which are not in good condition, are also of various dates. Those of the lower parts of the church proper should be contemporary with its building, even though the style in the south aisle is more old-fashioned, those of the upper storey are of the fifteenth century, and the sanctuary was redecorated in the seventeenth century. Of the other buildings of the Metropolis the west court was largely re- built in the eighteenth century and the north court may be Byzantine, though much altered afterwards. A small museum houses fragments of sculpture and inscriptions that have been found in Mistra.

The little church of the Evangelistria, which has been restored, is of elongated cross in square plan and was built probably about the end of the fourteenth century, but the annexes on the south and the west seem a little later. In style it has much of the Middle Byzantine about it, though the narthex is two-storeyed and the eaves of the dome are prettily varied. Inside the carving is well preserved, if inferior in quality, but very little of the original painting has survived.

The double monastery of the Brontocheion contained the churches of the Saints Theodore and of Afendiko, each with its complement of cells, refectory and kitchen, now in ruins. The church of the Saints Theodore, built before 1296 and much restored, is probably the oldest in Mistra. Its plan recalls Daphni, with wide central dome supported by eight piers or columns, but the corner bays have been converted into chapels and originally there was no narthex. The exterior has lost some of its showi- ness; at the east end there were bands of marble or decorative brickwork between the courses of cloisonné masonry, and the inset bowls have disappeared. The paintings inside the main part of the church are badly preserved, those of the eastern chapels in better condition; mostly they are the late thirteenth or early fourteenth century, except in the north- east chapel, where they cannot be before 1425. The church of Afendiko (or the Hodegetria), also much restored, was built rather before 1311. Its plan is basilical on the ground floor but cross in square in the upper storey, and is the earliest example of this fusion at Mistra. Besides the central dome there are four minor domes at the corners of the church and another in the middle of the narthex, which also has towers projecting at its ends. To make the effect more complex porticos and chapels were from the first annexed on all sides except the east and there was a three-storey belfry at the south-west. As often at Mistra the external masonry was of rubble, punctuated by courses of bricks, a cheaper but also more picturesque technique than cloisonné. Inside, the lower part of the walls was faced with marble, but this like most of the carved stonework has gone—only one of the handsome leaf capitals is genuine. Of the paintings some good pieces survive; they are by several hands of the fourteenth and earlier fifteenth centuries.

The street up to the Palace leads through the restored Monemvasia gate, an undistinguished vaulted passage in the wall, and arrives at the courtyard, the only sizable piece of level ground in the city. Here the Turks had the market and near the end of their tenure built a mosque. The Palace is an impressive ruin, still very little restored, and seems to have been built in three stages. The oldest part is the easternmost block with a vaulted hall, a low upper storey and at the end a tower. With this goes a detached kitchen block and tower further west. The date should be very soon after 1262, though because of the pointed windows some experts think this first palace the work of the Franks; if so, the wall of the upper town should also be Frankish. A century or so later the two early blocks were joined by an annexe for the court retinue and the range was extended west by an imposing residence for the Despot (or Governor) and his family, notable for the long arcade supporting a first-floor balcony on its outer face. The four-storey west wing, which included throne and reception rooms, is a more coherent monumental addition of the first half of the fifteenth century and even makes an architectural feature of the eight chimney stacks at the back. Originally it had a portico on its courtyard front and the outside walls were stuccoed and painted to imitate cloisonné masonry, a practice revived in some modern Greek churches. The flamboyant windows are presumably Italian in inspiration, and altogether the effect of the Palace is Western rather than Byzantine.

The Nauplia gate stands beyond the Palace. From outside it there is a good view of the west wall of the city, which in places is still 40 feet high. The north wall of the lower town, at the foot of the hill, also has some fine stretches. These fortifications are in the main Byzantine, under strong Frankish influence; they were repaired of course by the Turks, but except for some towers hardly altered.

Ayia Sophia, the palace church, built around 1350 and much restored, is of greatly lengthened cross in square type with a low dome on the narthex and a full set of annexes. On the north there were a projecting chapel, a light portico and a belfry, on the west an exonarthex and chapels, and on the south a gallery and another chapel. The outside is faced with cloisonné masonry and ornamental brickwork. Inside the carved decoration is badly damaged; a little painting remains in the main church, more in the two eastern chapels. The ruins of a monastic refectory can be seen to the west of the church and a fairly well preserved cistern to the north.

From here one can go up to the castle, which with its keep, inner court and outer court is basically Frankish, occasionally repaired and modernised by the Turks, who also added the round tower and buttresses at the north-east. Inside there are ruins of a pair of chapels, Turkish houses and cisterns. The castle is disappointing, except for the views it gives.

Between the church of Ayia Sophia and that of St Nicholas (of the seventeenth century and restored to illustrate the degeneration of the Late Byzantine style both in architecture and painting) there are ruins of many houses which go back to the fifteenth century or earlier. These Byzantine houses vary in plan from simple rectangles to complexes of two or more wings. Usually upper floors had balconies supported by corbelling, outer walls were of rubble mixed with brick and strengthened by arches, windows too were arched, and there was some decorative brickwork of the kind used in the churches. Later work is of course frequent but, whether repairs or new building, tends to be coarser in both style and technique. The finest and one of the best preserved of these houses is the so-called 'Little Palace', built and enlarged from the thirteenth to the fifteenth centuries. Much more typical examples of this period are the 'Frangopoulos house' beyond Pantanassa and the 'Lascaris house' near St Christopher's; the names, of course, are modern.

The convent of Pantanassa, which has been maintained by a diligent colony of nuns, is exceedingly picturesque in its architecture, setting and sense of placid life, and to be enjoyed most fully should be visited after an exhausting tour of ruins. The church was built in the 1420's by the minister Frangopoulos and has survived with less loss than any other church in Mistra—the west portico has been removed, the dome rebuilt and the internal fittings from time to time renewed. Its plan, much like that of Afendiko but more elongated, is basilical below and cross in square above, and it has the same arrangement of domes. The outside is richly decorated, with Italian influence in the pointed arches of the east end and still more in the belfry. Inside, the original effect has been spoilt by later replacements, but the paintings are unusually complete, those of the vaults and the galleries being of the fifteenth century and the others mainly of the seventeenth.

The little church called Peribleptos, built early in the fourteenth century, is closer than any other church in Mistra to the Middle Byzantine tradition. Its exterior is soberly cloisonné, its plan a slightly lengthened cross in square, though because of the site the narthex is on the south side and the annexes—here three chapels—are set obliquely at the east and south-west. The paintings inside, damaged and in places restored, are by various hands of the earlier fourteenth century and, especially since the dome has survived, give an unusually good idea of the original total effect. In this part of Mistra there are several good chapels, more or less restored. Ayi Taxiarchai (the Holy Brigadiers or Archangels) is unusual in having three apses at its east end. St George's has decorative brickwork, and so has St Anne's. St Christopher's is distinguished by paintings in a fourteenth-century style. St John's, just outside the city wall, was built around 1400, and is notable for both architecture and paintings; it is perhaps the most interesting and least typical of the chapels. About 200 yards south and still outside the wall are the ruins of houses of the Turkish period, of which one belonged to the Krevatas family, the richest in the Peloponnese till they imprudently committed themselves to the revolt of 1770.

Monemvasia

It is about 60 miles by road from Sparta to Monemvasia on the east coast. There are two routes. The better starts on the road to Yithion and after about 15 miles branches off left to pass through Skala and Molaoi. The other route, slower but very fair, leaves Sparta by the Tripolis highway, just after the bridge turns right, leads on through Goritsa to Geraki (Yeraki), and from there goes south to Vlachioti, which is some 15 miles short of Molaoi on the road (already mentioned) from Skala.

Monemvasia (the ancient Minoa) is a precipitous rock, about a mile long and over 900 feet high, which once was a peninsula and is now an island, though joined to the mainland by a causeway. It was an excellent refuge, never—so far as is known—taken by assault, but inconveniently remote and without good harbourage. So in the Late Bronze Age and Classical times the chief place of the district was Epidaurus Limera, of which there are unimportant remains 3 miles up the coast (1½ miles north of the road where it turns inland), but Monemvasia has had importance when a naval power needed a foothold in the south-east Peloponnese. The rock was first settled by refugees from the Slav invasions, probably in the seventh century A.D., capitulated to the Franks in 1248 after a three-year blockade, was reoccupied by the Byzantines in 1262, accepted the protection of the Pope in 1460 and of the Venetians in 1463, was ceded to the Turks in 1540, enjoyed a second Venetian suzerainty from 1690 to 1715, and was the first stronghold to fall to the Greek rebels in 1821. During the Middle Ages its situation saved it from the exactions of the various powers to which it was subordinate, and it had a flourishing commerce in—among other commodities—the wine called Malmsey in English by a corruption of 'Monemvasia'. This prosperity declined after the fifteenth century and the independence of Greece brought inevitable decay.

The town is in two parts, both fortified, the upper and presumably older on the top of the rock and the lower (which goes back anyhow to the second Byzantine period) on the steep slope that runs down at the south. The walls, badly designed for artillery though in practice adequate, seem to be Turkish of the sixteenth century (with a later western gate) but perhaps stand on Byzantine foundations; the south-west bastion of the lower circuit was rebuilt by the Venetians around 1700. In the lower town, much of which is ruined, many of the houses have clumsy Renaissance details which suggest that they are Venetian and there are some interesting churches. The oldest is the Elkomenos in the main square, a basilica with central dome, which may have been built in the fourteenth century but was restored in 1697, and there are others built about that time: all are abnormal and show more or less Italian influence. The upper town is completely ruined. At the summit of the plateau there are the remains of a fort, probably of the first Byzantine period, and on the edge of the northern cliff the fine church of Ayia Sophia is especially impressive when approached from the east. This church, built in the fourteenth century and considerably restored, resembles in plan the Saints Theodore in Mistra: its dome has eight supports, but the narthex is two-storeyed and a portico was annexed on the south. Recently some early paintings have been uncovered inside it.

Geraki

Geraki (or Yeraki) on the byroad from Sparta to Monemvasia is not well known. The modern village is at the site of the ancient city of Geron-thrae and there are ruins of a medieval castle and town on a steep hill a mile or so east.

Geronthrae had some importance. Prehistoric remains have turned up, it flourished in Hellenic and Roman times, a basilical church of the fifth century A.D. has been excavated, round the modern village there are churches (some restored) which are said to date from the eleventh century on, and Geraki was one of the twelve original baronies of the Frankish Peloponnese. The best and probably the oldest church is Ayios Sozon. The acropolis, to the north of the village, was defended by a rough wall of uncertain but ancient date; parts of it survive and there are signs of medieval repair.

At the other site the castle was built by the Franks in 1254, passed to the Byzantines hardly much later than 1262, and is last mentioned as a garrisoned place in 1467. Some good stretches of its wall are still standing. On the west slope of the castle hill there are remains of a town and other buildings extended along the ridge to the south. Again there are churches, several of them restored. St George's, inside the walls of the castle, is notable for interior stonework of Frankish style and others show traces of painting (as do some of the churches of the village). The dating of this town is uncertain. One would expect it to follow the castle, but some authorities think this too late for all the churches.

9 · Messenia

Messenia is an agreeable region and not much visited. It too has its fertile plain, about 20 miles long, stretching northwards from Kalamata at the head of the gulf. The easiest approach is from Arcadia, by the highway from Megalopolis. Another route, most of it good, is by the coastal road from Patras and Pyrgos, turning inland either 5 miles north of Kyparissia or at Pylos. The direct road to Kalamata over the mountains from Sparta is rough though scenic, and the road from Yithion through Areopolis patchy. The most comfortable places to stay at are Kalamata and Pylos. Messenian (or Kalamata) black olives are reckoned the best in Greece.

In Mycenaean times, so a recent survey suggests, Messenia was quite as densely populated as the Argolid; of the hundred and more tholos tombs known in Greece nearly half were here, including the earliest; and Homer's catalogue of the Greek forces at Troy makes the kingdom of Pylos militarily almost as powerful as that of Mycenae. In the Early Iron Age we hear of a unified kingdom of Messenia, which was conquered and annexed by the Spartans in the later eighth century. Though rebellious enough, the Messenians did not recover their independence till 369 B.C., when the Thebans broke the Spartan empire. There is nothing distinctive about the later history of the region, except in its special interest to the Venetians for calling stations on their sea route to the East.

Kalamata

Kalamata, the ancient Pharae, is mentioned by Homer and Mycenaean tombs have been found near-by. Later it was a Classical and Byzantine city. It was captured by the Franks in A.D. 1205, recovered by the Byzantines soon after 1425, and held by the Venetians for a little while before the Turkish conquest about 1470 and again from 1685 to 1715. The ruined castle on the ancient acropolis, mediocre but improved with trees and a cafe, is basically Frankish of the thirteenth century with high keep, inner enclosure and outer enclosure, but the outer wall and much else was rebuilt or remodelled by the Venetians around 1700, even though the situation did not allow satisfactory defence against the new artillery. In the wall north-east of the keep there are stretches of Byzantine work both earlier and later than the Frankish, in the keep itself part of a small Byzantine church is immured (probably of the eleventh or twelfth century), and here and there ancient blocks are re-used. In and around the town several other churches of the same date survive, more or less renovated. The finest for its ornamental brickwork is that of St Charalambos, now incorporated as a sort of crypt at the east end of the church in the public cemetery, which incidentally displays some fine modern monuments; but there is a more immediate pleasure in the cruciform Holy Apostles by the bazaar, with a larger seventeenth century extension to the west and an inappropriate belfry. Kalamata is, though, more remarkable for its liqueurs, and a hotel by the shore served the best 'mezes' we have had recently in Greece.

Messene (Ithome)   (*Fig.* 25)

Mt Ithome is the landmark of Messenia. Near its top was the ancient city of Messene, now sometimes miscalled Ithome to avoid confusion with the new Messene (formerly Nisi) which is a dozen miles distant. From Kalamata one takes the road to this modern Messene, turns right for Lambena 7 miles away, and there branches left along a fairish track that climbs in 5 miles to Mavrommati, the village inside the limits of old Messene. The track goes on, forking left outside the Arcadian Gate and deteriorating, and in about 6 miles comes down to Meligala. Lambena is connected by a fair road with Goukalaiika 4 miles away on the high-road from Megalopolis to Kalamata; and Meligala is linked both with this highroad and the cross route to Kyparissia.

In earlier centuries the Messenians had used Ithome as a stronghold, but it was the Thebans in 369 B.C. who founded the city of Messene, to serve (like Megalopolis) as a centre of a new state and a barrier to Spartan aggression. Though the Greek excavation has not gone far, it seems that Messene did not survive into the Middle Ages, and the names of both city and mountain were forgotten.

The fortifications were planned with strict regard to the lie of the land and on the north, where they have often lost little more than the parapet, are extremely impressive, running down from the peak to the Arcadian Gate (with inner courtyard) and up again to the north-west corner. The northern part of the west wall is also well preserved. To see these

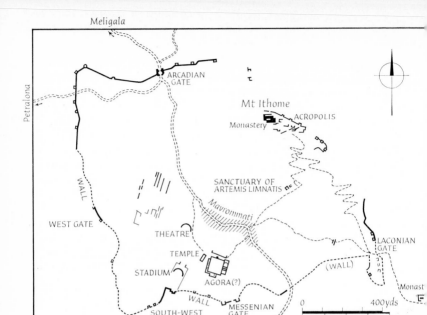

Fig. 25. Messene.

stretches most conveniently one follows the track through the village to the Arcadian Gate (unless of course one comes up from Meligala) and afterwards takes the track for Petralona, which branches west just inside the gate. Some of the towers of the wall are easy to reach, but a wider reconnaissance needs more than sandals and bare legs. Most archaeologists put these fortifications about the 360's B.C., though a few think their design too advanced and prefer a Hellenistic date at least for part of them. To be honest, not much is known about the exact chronology of Greek defences.

Not so much of the space within the walls was built up and still less has been explored. The principal remains are in the basin below the track, reached by paths at each end of the village, but only the so-called Agora has any particular interest. This is a rectangular colonnaded court, bordered by buildings of various purposes: the most notable are on the west a temple of Artemis with its entrance at the side, at the south what seems to be an official residence, and on the east a square room with benches round three walls—perhaps a council chamber—and beyond a stairway a very small enclosed theatre. This complex is probably Hellenistic, though remodelled in Roman times. Among other ruins there are traces of a proper theatre and a stadium.

At the bend of the village street a path goes up eastwards, forking left for the peak and right for the big monastery of Vourkano. On the peak there are traces of fortifications, a little monastery perhaps as early as the sixteenth century, and the view. The larger monastery, an offshoot of the other and about ¾ mile south-east of it, was built in 1712 and for its period is creditable.

About ¾ mile west of Meligala, just before Neochori on the way up to Mavrommati and on the right of the road, where it cross the Mavrozoumenos river, there stands a three-way bridge, ancient in its lower parts though repaired above in the Middle Ages and later. Presumably it was built in the fourth or third century B.C. as part of the road system for Messene. It is interesting mainly for its plan and as evidence that the Greeks understood the arch, though they rarely used it.

Korone (Coron)

Korone or Coron, on a cape facing east across the Messenian Gulf, is 32 miles from Kalamata by a fair road and 20 from Methone by another that may be impassable. In Classical times Asine (as it was then called) was a small walled city and the site was inhabited for at least part of the Byzantine period, when refugees from ancient Korone—at Petalidhi 15 miles back on the Kalamata road—brought the name of their city with them. The new Korone fell to the Franks in 1205, but next year was annexed by the Venetians who made it one of their principal strongholds. The Turks took the place in 1500, the Venetians recovered it in 1685, the Turks came back in 1715, the French expelled them in 1828, and the Germans were in occupation during the last war.

The fortifications are impressive. In general the circuit, with entrance on the south side, is Venetian of the thirteenth century, modernised in the fifteenth; the east end with its two bastions (one blown up by the Germans) may be Turkish reconstruction of the sixteenth century; and the western defences are Venetian improvements of about 1700. The octagonal tower in the upper enclosure, which now contains a monastery, is earlier and Turkish. The cross wall between the upper and lower enclosures is the old outer wall of the Byzantine fortress, built as often elsewhere with random use of earlier materials. West of the main gate (probably of 1209) and in the lower of the pair of bastions at the north-east of the fortress there are courses of large ancient blocks, either re-used or surviving parts of the Classical defences, which must have stood on much the same line.

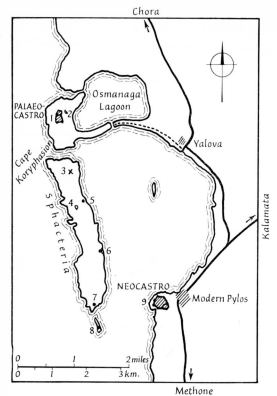

Methone (Modon)

From modern Pylos a fair road leads in 8 miles to Methone (or Modon) and there may be a rough road of about 20 miles from Korone. Methone was a fortified town in ancient and Byzantine times, though how continuously is not known. It was a pirate base when the Venetians sacked it in A.D. 1125, and they annexed it permanently in 1206. Like Korone it was strategically important as a naval station and profited also from pilgrims to the Holy Land, so long as their conveyance was the monopoly of the Serene Republic. The place was stormed by the Turks in 1500, retaken by the Venetians in 1686, lost again to the Turks in 1715, liberated by the French in 1828, and garrisoned by the Italians in the recent war. All these occupants have left their traces. The elaborate outer defences at the north, across the neck of the peninsula, are a good example of artillery fortification: they are mainly Venetian of 1494, though the forward structures at each end belong to their second tenure and the entrance bridge was rebuilt by the French. The less exposed eastern and western curtain walls are mainly early Venetian, presumably following the course of the ancient fortifications, which are indeed visible in a breach at the north-west and in the first tower on the east (beside the beach). On the islet at the south the octagonal tower in two stages is a Turkish reconstruction, more elegant than effective, done soon after 1500, and below water remains of the old mole can be seen running from it towards the north-east. The sanding up against the east wall, which makes a good beach for bathers, has been caused by the modern mole further north. This serves the present settlement, to which in 1828 the French removed the inhabitants of the old and now almost vanished town within the fortifications.

Modern Pylos (Neocastro)   (*Fig.* 26)

The pleasant little town now officially named Pylos stands at the south corner of the bay of Navarino. This bay, protected by the long island of Sphacteria, is the best natural harbour of the western Peloponnese, though its hinterland has never been large enough to allow a busy port. Its fame comes from two naval episodes, both significant and both acci-dental. The earlier, of 425 B.C., belongs to the next section. The later, in A.D. 1827, was a turning point in the Greek War of Independence. The three interested neutrals—Britain, France and Russia—had agreed to recognise the Greek insurgents and sent combined flotillas to enforce an armistice. These found the Turkish fleet in the bay and after some provocation destroyed it—to the embarrassment of the British govern-ment and the glory of the admirals, commemorated in cafes and a handsome series of postage stamps. The wrecks of Turkish ships can still, it is said, be seen in the clear water.

The castle above the modern town is unusually homogeneous and well preserved. It was built by the Turks in 1573 to secure the bay against Venetian attack and perhaps because the northern channel was becoming too shallow. In 1686 it fell to the Venetians, in 1715 to the Turks, and in 1828 to the French, who moved the inhabitants to the town outside. Later the castle was used as barracks and a prison. The low fortifications were designed for artillery, though not very competently, and consist of a strong hexagonal fort at the top and two smaller forts by the shore, all connected by an irregular curtain. There has not been much remodelling, though in the main fort the arched openings for musketeers have been walled up to make prison cells and the central space divided into separate yards. On the exposed sides of this fort the system of defence is admirably clear, with the cannon embrasures placed to command the carefully graded slope of the glacis (now planted with trees) and to enfilade the dry ditch in front. Lower down the hill a mosque has been converted into a pleasant church by simply lopping the minaret and refurnishing inside.

Classical Pylos (Palaeocastro)   (*Fig.* 26)

The old castle or Palaeocastro was on Cape Koryphasion at the north end of the bay, which in ancient times did not include the present lagoon of Osmanaga. By the fifth century B.C. the place was called Pylos, but though naturally strong was unoccupied in 425 B.C., when the Athenian and Spartan leagues were fighting the Peloponnesian War. That summer an Athenian fleet put in at Pylos because of bad weather and left a small garrison on the cape. Violation of their territory and the danger that rebellious Messenians would rally there provoked the Spartans to attack in force and when assault failed they settled down to a blockade, both from the land side and from the island of Sphacteria, where they put a detachment of 420 highly trained infantry with their batmen. What had started as a casual incident turned into a major test of strength. The Athenians reinforced their garrison and being better sailors took control of the sea, so that the Spartan detachment in turn was blockaded. Sphacteria is rough, barren and short of water, and Athenian skirmishers were landed on it to harass the heavily armed enemy. So after ten weeks the Spartans on the island surrendered. Though these losses seem negligible they were serious for the Spartans, since of the 292 survivors 120 were from the small ruling caste, and further the demonstration that Spartans too preferred dishonour to death had a powerful effect both at Athens and in the rest of Greece. The Athenians held Pylos for another sixteen years. Later, after the liberation of Messenia in 369 B.C., a small fortified town was established on the cape, which probably lasted till the Slav invasion of the late sixth century A.D. Before long the site had a new name of Slav origin—Avarinos, corrupted into Navarinos and Italianised as Navarino—but there seems to have been no reoccupation till in the late thirteenth century the Franks built a castle on the peak and a small town grew up below. The Venetians bought the place in 1423 and the Turks succeeded them in 1500. With the creation of Neocastro in 1573, Palaeocastro ceased to be important, but it was not completely deserted till the eighteenth century. Building stone was shipped away much longer.

The principal remains are those of the Frankish castle at the top of the hill; it rests in part on an older wall and there is later Venetian and Turkish work. At the foot on the north and the west some stretches of good masonry are probably from the fortifications of the fourth century B.C. A rough barrier of big unhewn blocks to the north may be an original Athenian defence of 425. Nearby is the entrance to the so-called Cave of Nestor, a vast chamber well hung with stalactites. Pausanias in the second century A.D. was told among other stories that Nestor stabled his cattle here. Neolithic and later sherds have been found inside.

This Pylos is in itself a site of only moderate interest, but it has the charm of remoteness and a special significance for willing readers of Thucydides. A track leads to within a mile of the place round the north shore of the bay, branching off from the road to Chora and Kyparissia, but cars are liable to stick in the sand. It is better to hire a small boat in modern Pylos and, if one wishes, visit Sphacteria too, though its attractions are mainly sentimental. The old fort at the north end, where finally the Spartans surrendered, was destroyed in the last war but memorials to heroes of the War of Independence are distributed along the length of the island.

Mycenaean Pylos (Epano Englianos) (*Fig.* 27)

About 10 miles along the road from modern Pylos to Chora and Kyparissia the low hill of Epano Englianos rises up on the left. The site was occupied already in the Middle Bronze Age and in the sixteenth century B.C.—to judge by the gateway and a stretch of wall at the northeast—the settlement was fortified. Of this phase some house walls survive at the east in the filling of a hollow, but most of the buildings and the fortifications were swept away in the early thirteenth century, when the hilltop was cleared and levelled for a large palace (defended, improbable as it may seem, only by the banked hillside) and lesser folk were moved to a new suburb below. All this was destroyed by fire about 1200 B.C., at much the same time as the palaces of Tiryns and Mycenae. Afterwards the site was and stayed deserted, though because of stone-robbing and cultivation the remains of buildings stand nowhere more than 4 feet high.

Fortunately, even the existence of this palace was unknown until in 1939 the Americans began work here. Their excavation, resumed in

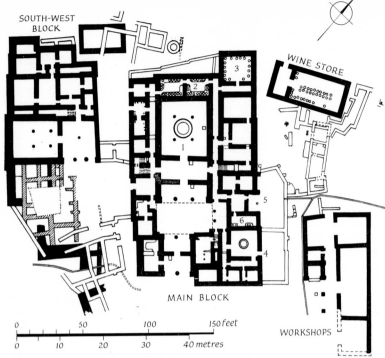

Fig. 27. **Epano Englianos** (Pylos), Mycenaean Palace. 1, 'megaron'. 2–3, store rooms with bases of jars. 4, separate suite ('Queen's rooms'). 5, separate suite (King's rooms). 6, bathroom.
By courtesy of C. W. Blegen

1952, has been both skilful and systematic and is being followed by conscientious study and publication. So for archaeologists this is the most informative of Mycenaean palaces and, though the roof erected over the remains is panoramically distracting, it allows friable floors and walls to be left open to view. The finds are divided provisionally between the National Museum at Athens and the local museum at Chora, $2\frac{1}{2}$ miles north of Epano Englianos.

According to Homer, at the time of the Trojan War Nestor, the ruler of at least western Messenia, had his palace at 'sandy' Pylos near the shore. Since the ruin at Epano Englianos, while not on a sandy site, is so far the only Mycenaean palace in the region and near one of the places called Pylos in Classical times, it is now often dubbed Homer's, Nestor's or Blegen's Pylos, according to the speaker's historical prejudice and sense of propriety. Incidentally, by the first century B.C. scholars were already disputing about the location of the Pylos mentioned by Homer, though they of course did not have the benefit of archaeology.

Entry to the main building of the palace is through a double porch with one column on each side. On its left a side door leads into two minor rooms, presumably a steward's office, since nearly a thousand clay tablets were found here, inscribed (as these Linear B Tablets usually are) with lists of commodities and workers. Beyond this porch is a shallow court, facing the grand porch of the megaron. It leads through an ante-room to the principal chamber with central hearth, four columns round it to support the roof, and on the right a space marked out for—presumably—a throne. This is very like Tiryns. A curious feature on the right of each of the two doorways to the megaron and on the left of the doorway of the outer porch is a low platform; guesses at their purpose are stands for guards, torches or (inevitably) objects of cult. Against each side of the megaron ran a corridor, that on the left later partitioned off; beyond them and at the back were store rooms, some (as in other parts of the palace) still containing the bases of the jars that were there when the palace was burnt down. The east corner of the block was more important and had its own two-columned porch at the side of the internal court. On the right a narrow door was the only entrance to a suite which included an elaborately decorated squarish room with central hearth and beyond it a walled yard or garden. On the left of the porch and round the corner a short passage led to another secluded group of rooms and another walled enclosure. One of these rooms had set in its floor a terracotta bath and two big jars, all containing typical Mycenaean drinking cups, whether to rinse or refresh the bather. Where the water was heated is not clear—perhaps in the yard which had a piped supply. The excavators suggest that the suite with a bath was for the king to retire to and the other the queen's reception rooms. Still, the palace was not all on one level. The megaron itself is thought to have had a gallery round its walls and a lantern to let out the smoke in the centre, and the surrounding rooms certainly had an upper floor—11 feet above the ground floor, as has been calculated from the space available for the staircases and the height of surviving risers. Since the debris below contained fragments of such objects as ivory combs, these upper rooms were probably the private apartments.

The south-west block, to the left of the main building and reaching to the edge of the hilltop, was put up rather earlier but continued in use. It has suffered badly from stone-robbing and erosion. The principal room had four internal columns, not placed centrally; presumably there was a hearth and conceivably more columns towards the back. The porch, which was set sideways, had two columns at the entrance and another standing centrally behind but hard to explain functionally. It is also hard to explain why there should be in effect two palaces side by side, unless perhaps the south-west block was kept for banqueting.

On the other side of the main building and projecting forward is an irregular block comprising workrooms, probably an armoury, and perhaps a chapel. Behind is a row of small rooms and a big wine store. The palace was remarkably well stocked in wine and oil and in crockery. The walls of the principal buildings were for the first storey mainly of rubble, faced on the exterior with ashlar; a small stretch survives in the main block near the north-west corner of the 'king's yard'. The upper storey was of mud brick. Both stone and brick were reinforced by a heavy timber framework; the gaps left by its burning can be seen here and there. The roofs were flat. Interior walls and floors were stuccoed and, if important, painted. For floors formal patterns were usual, but the decoration of walls was more ambitious with such subjects as musicians and pink griffins. In various places—for instance the hearth of the big megaron—several successive coats of stucco can be seen. Columns were of wood on stone footings and, as is shown by imprints in the stucco of the floor laid round them, they were fluted. In spite of later alterations it is plain that the component blocks of the palace were planned as unities and should exemplify the mature principles of Mycenaean architecture. In the main block the central suite (the megaron) seems intended to be axially symmetrical, though its outer facade is unbalanced and the porch eccentric. Other irregularities may be less deliberate, such as the setting back of stretches of the outer wall, the obliquity of the cross-walls of the megaron itself, and the quite unrelated distortion of the chequer pattern of its floor. It looks as if Mycenaean builders and their patrons had erratic standards of accuracy.

Between the workshop and wine store blocks a water main (with settling basins) was brought in, but its branches do not seem to have extended through the palace. Its course has been traced to the north-east end of the hill and must have come from further away; the likeliest spot is a spring more than half a mile to the north. Since the system was gravity and not pressure, it must have crossed the hollow by an aqueduct, presumably—for want of stone foundations—of wood. A hundred yards beyond the old north-east gate is a tholos tomb which looks brand new, and indeed its upper part is.

10 · Elis

Elis, much of it flat and fertile, is the north-west part of the Peloponnese. It is traversed by the highway from Patras through Pyrgos to Kyparissia; another main road runs from Tripolis through Vlacherna and Olympia to Pyrgos; and there is the route, part bad and part good, from Andritsena to Pyrgos. There are good hotels at Olympia and one at Kyllene.

Though inhabited from early times Elis remained backward, a country of big landowners with very little taste for urban life, and it is fitting that the miserable remains of their capital city (just beyond Bouchioti, 7 miles east of Gastouni) are grown over again almost as soon as excavated. The one period when this region became important was under the Franks, whose ties—personal, military and economic—were with Western Europe, and Elis was the nearest part of the Peloponnese: perhaps too the landscape reminded them of Flanders.

Olympia   (*Fig.* 28, *Plate* 12)

For the northern tourist Olympia has the most congenial setting of any major site of ancient Greece. It lies in the well-watered valley of the Alpheus which flows, even in summer, between comfortable wooded hills. This rural landscape never supported any sizable town and it was perhaps because the local community of Pisa was politically insignificant that the other Greeks accepted its Olympic Games as the most important festival in their calendar. Traditionally these games were founded in 776 B.C. as a small one-day meeting for the surrounding countryside, but within two centuries competitors and spectators were coming from all parts of the Greek world, most of them camping out in the valley and catered for by food vendors, fortune-tellers, pedlars, charlatans and propagandists. The programme now lasted for five days; to the original one-stade race (about 210 yards) there were added from time to time a two-stade race, a long distance race, boxing, wrestling, all-in wrestling, the pentathlon (which comprised a one-stade race, long jump, throwing

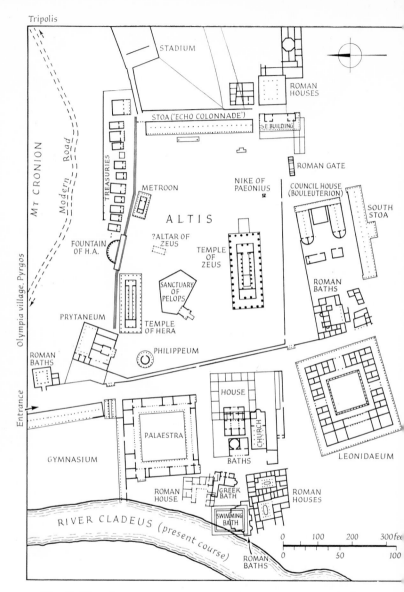

Tripolis

STADIUM

ROMAN
HOUSES

STOA ('ECHO COLONNADE')

SE BUILDING

ROMAN GATE

TREASURIES

Mt CRONION

Modern Road

METROON

NIKE OF
PAEONIUS

COUNCIL HOUSE
(BOULEUTERION)

SOUTH
STOA

ALTIS

FOUNTAIN
OF H.A.

?ALTAR OF
ZEUS

Olympia village. Pyrgos

TEMPLE
OF
ZEUS

PRYTANEUM

SANCTUARY
OF PELOPS

ROMAN
BATHS

TEMPLE
OF HERA

ROMAN
BATHS

PHILIPPEUM

Entrance

HOUSE

CHURCH

PALAESTRA

BATHS

GYMNASIUM

LEONIDAEUM

ROMAN
HOUSE

GREEK
BATH

ROMAN
HOUSES

SWIMMING
BATH

RIVER CLADEUS (present course)

0   100   200   300 feet

0   50   100

ROMAN
BATHS

Fig. 28. Olympia.

Plate 12. Model of Olympia, once in Berlin. Views from south-east and north-east.

the javelin, throwing the discus and wrestling), a two-stade race in armour and races for horses and chariots (the owner and not the driver taking the credit); in the first seven of these events there were also competitions for boys. Entries were made individually and the prizes were wreaths of wild olive, but the victor also received enormous prestige and often material benefits in his home city. Because of expense, competitors were mostly upper class till the fourth century B.C., when professionalism came in and—so it is often said—lowered the sporting tone; but long before that the caustic philosopher Xenophanes had expressed his opinion on the rewards accepted and expected by amateurs. The Olympic Games continued through Roman times (when in A.D. 67 the Emperor Nero at a specially postponed meeting was content to win seven events) and they were finally suppressed for their paganism in 393.

Although, when properly established, the festival was held only for a few days every four summers, its prestige and the crowds it drew induced other Greek states to advertise themselves at Olympia by showy buildings and dedications, particularly when they had a victory over other Greeks to celebrate; and there were of course the statues put up by or for winners in the Games. The sanctuary too, without any famous oracle or object of pilgrimage, collected enough one way or another for some capital expenditure of its own. So by the fifth century B.C. the Altis (as the sacred precinct was called) was becoming full and, though old structures and monuments might decay or be cleared away and Roman conquerors carted off scores of statues, till the second century A.D. blank spaces were soon reoccupied. Troubled times followed, and in A.D. 267 the barbarous Herulians broke into Greece, sacking among other places Athens and Corinth. They did not reach Olympia, but the authorities there prepared to defend as much as they could and hurriedly walled in the Temple of Zeus, the Council House and the South Stoa; to get stone for this wall (which till recently was thought to be Byzantine) they pulled down most of the surrounding buildings. As for the temple, the Emperor Theodosius II is said to have had it burnt in 426, though it was as unusual then as now for a government to destroy its own property and the remains do not show the effects of any serious fire. Anyhow, the columns and pedimental sculpture needed an earthquake, probably in the sixth century, to bring them down and afterwards floods and landslides buried Olympia under some 10 to 20 feet of sand, gravel and mud. Even the name was forgotten.

The site was rediscovered in 1766 by Richard Chandler, who saw the

cella wall of the temple projecting above the plain; a few pieces of sculpture (now in the Louvre) were unearthed in 1829 by savants attached to
the French military force which had been sent to support the Greek
rebellion; but it was left to the new German Empire to demonstrate its
love of culture by the grand excavations of 1875–81. Well organised
and executed and remarkably successful these set a new standard for
work in Greece. In 1936 the Germans began to excavate again and their
work continues still with success.

The usual approach to the site is from the modern village. The visitor
follows the Tripolis road down to the river Cladeus, which joins the
Alpheus in another few hundred yards. Across the bridge and on the
right is the entry to the site and an open space where there once stood a
little modern altar, at which before recent Olympiads the sacred flame
was lit with supposedly Grecian antics, and a stele in memory of their
founder, de Coubertin; these monuments have been moved to a grove,
further along the road and beyond the stadium, named grandiloquently
the International Olympic Academy. At the entrance to the ancient site
there are visible on the right the re-erected rows of small columns of the
Palaestra and the Gymnasium, built in the third and second centuries
B.C. Half-right through the trees there are glimpses of the temples of
Hera and of Zeus. In ancient times the Altis contained a grove of plane
trees; the Germans after their first excavations planted it with pines,
now judiciously thinned and giving shade and scenic variety to what
could otherwise be a torrid expanse of featureless ruins. Going through
the gateway in the Altis wall one comes to the Heraeum (or temple of
Hera), the earliest reasonably preserved example of Doric architecture.
It was built soon after 600 B.C. The walls of the cella had one high course
of stone and were carried up in mud brick. The columns, two of which
have been re-erected, vary in their proportions, since originally many
(if not all) were of wood and the stone replacements made at various
times were in contemporary style: the holes cut in their faces were for
votive plaques. The entablature too was of wood. Inside this building
were found the colossal head of Hera from the cult statue and the
Hermes. Behind and on the right are the remains of the partly marble
Philippeum, notable for its Corinthian capitals and for being round; it
was begun by Philip of Macedon about 337 B.C. to celebrate his dominance of Greece. Beyond the Heraeum in an excavators' pit the conscientious tourist can speculate on the foundations of two apsidal houses of
the Middle Bronze Age. Next, along the north side of the Altis appears
the brick core of the exedra of Herodes Atticus, a fountain lavishly

adorned with bad statues (mostly preserved and in the Museum) and the first supplier of piped water in Olympia; till then—A.D. 160—the Altis had relied on wells. Further on the ruins of several treasuries stand on a terrace; they belonged, so Pausanias relates, to Sicyon, Megara, Epidamnus in Albania, Sybaris and Metapontum in South Italy, Syracuse, Gela and Selinus in Sicily, Cyrene in Libya and Byzantium. Ahead a vaulted tunnel of Roman date leads into the Stadium, a monument to the bulldozer, which cleared out the hollow and rebuilt the south bank. The starting grooves for the runners' feet are original. In its present form the Stadium is true to the remodelling of the fourth century B.C., with earth banks for some 45,000 spectators and a natural track that was cleaned up for each festival; in races of more than one stade (the length of the track of what for that reason was called the stadium) there was a post at the other end round which the runners turned. The earlier stadium lay about 85 yards further west, starting in the sanctuary; on its bank the recent excavations found hundreds of pieces of armour, dedicated as trophies from Greek battles. The hippodrome, where the horse races were held, has been washed away. Coming back into the Altis and bearing left past the base of the Nike of Paeonius, the visitor may admire the huge platform of the Temple of Zeus, the patron deity of Olympia, with its column drums neatly tumbled by the earthquake. The stone, a shelly conglomerate, is one of the coarsest ever used by the ancient Greeks, but must have provided a good key for its stucco facing. Its date is around 460 B.C. Outside the Altis at the south-east there are brick-built ruins of Roman buildings, including Nero's house. To the south of the big temple stood the Council House, twin halls with apses at the west and going back to the sixth and fifth centuries B.C. Beyond was the so-called South Stoa of the fourth century B.C., now facing a high bank which shows in section the depth of deposit laid by medieval floods. To the south-west is the Leonidaeum, identified by an inscription and presumably an official hostel; it was built in the fourth century B.C. and remodelled in the second century A.D. To the north of the Leonidaeum among remains of Greek and Roman baths and Roman houses there stand out the walls of a Roman building, which was converted into a church in the fifth century A.D. It overlies the workshop of Phidias, where in the 430's that great sculptor constructed his statue of Olympian Zeus. Forty feet high and seated, with ivory flesh and drapery of gold sheeting, the thought of it makes many moderns blench; the ancients admired it vastly and probably with justice. It was removed to Constantinople by a Christian emperor and inevitably destroyed in a fire. Pieces of the moulds for the drapery were found recently in the workshop, and a small jug inscribed 'I belong to Phidias'. On the way back to the bridge those curious about ancient kilns can find two well preserved specimens of the fourth century A.D. and traces of earlier ones. The ascent of Mt Cronion, which rises above the site on the north, is a harmless exercise, but the view is spoilt by trees.

The Museum contains, though it cannot exhibit, nearly everything found at Olympia and should not be missed by anyone who has or professes the slightest interest in Greek art. Of the sculpture the lime-stone head of the cult statue of Hera from the Heraeum is provincial, probably Laconian, work of the early sixth century B.C. A half-size terracotta group of Zeus with Ganymede, of about 470 B.C., is notable because it still has its original colouring, though darkened by necessary preservatives. What cannot be overlooked are the pedimental sculpture and metopes of the temple of Zeus, carved about 460 B.C. and fairly complete. The East (or front) pediment, rather stiffly composed, represents a sacrifice before the chariot race in which Pelops won Oenomaus's daughter by bribing his charioteer; Zeus stands in the centre, guaranteeing scarcely fair play. The West pediment is less relevant to Olympia, but livelier; the drunken Centaurs break up the wedding feast of the Lapith king Pirithous and attack the women, while Apollo directs rescue in the centre. When admiring these masterpieces of early Classical sculpture, one should remember that they stood 60 feet above eye level and so detail needed to be bold and simple, and that strong colours covered hair, drapery, centaurs, horses and background; or, as an exercise in stylistic sense, one may detect the three Hellenistic or Roman replace-ments in the corners. That the team who carved the pediments did not work from detailed scale models is evident from the adjustments made to figures to fit them into the pedimental space and from the quite different treatments of the folds of drapery. The metopes, made up with casts of fragments in Paris, show twelve Labours of Heracles and are of the same date and style, though subtler. The developments of the next generation are displayed in another monument, the Nike carved by Paeonius, though the front and side views are not yet co-ordinated. From the side the ogival curves of the swirling skirt produce an illusion of motion, and in front the looped ridges across the right thigh make it appear more fully rounded than the naked left. For those who remember Thucydides the Nike was dedicated about 420 B.C. by the Messenians who settled in Naupactus. It stood in front of the temple of Zeus on a triangular pedestal some 30 feet high. The Hermes holding an infant

Dionysus may be an original by Praxiteles or an unusually fine Roman copy: certainly the high polish of the surface is unlike anything else of the mid fourth century B.C. Of the remaining sculptures a miserable bull from Herodes Atticus's exedra probably receives most homage. In their way the collection of bronze figurines, attachments and armour is equally remarkable. These begin in the eighth century B.C. and remain very numerous throughout the Archaic period. Miscellaneous curiosities include the helmet of Miltiades, Phidias's jug, and a 316-pound boulder which Bybon lifted with one hand over his head; all are certified by inscriptions.

In the village there is a little Museum of the History of the Modern Olympic Games, which it is kindest to describe as ingenuous; the tourists' bazaars and cafes revive the ancient spirit more faithfully; and the railway station is one no connoisseur should miss.

Medieval Monuments

At the south of *Gastouni*, which is a dozen miles from Pyrgos on the road to Patras, the church of the Panayia Katholiki is a good specimen of the Middle Byzantine style, comparable to Ayia Moni and Merbaka in the Argolid and perhaps to be dated just after 1150. It is of cross in square plan, with fine ornamental brickwork and inset bowls. Later a Gothic doorway was inserted and an annexe built on at the west. There has been some restoration.

Andravidha, 4 miles north on the highway, was the capital of the Frankish Peloponnese, but the only monument worth seeing is the east end of the ruined cathedral, a couple of blocks to the west of the main street. By Western standards it was small and the style is a severe but neat Gothic, though from the use of brick with stone the builders were local.

About 8 miles to the west *Chlemoutsi* (or Castle Tornese) is a landmark that stands out clearly. The castle stands 10 minutes walk from the modern village (half-way between Killini and Loutra Killini) and there are roads through Neochori from Lechena (just north of Andravidha) and from Gastouni. Chlemoutsi is well preserved and as impressive near to as from a distance. It was built by the Franks in 1220–3 as the castle of the Prince of Achaea, was acquired by the Byzantines in 1427, and duly passed on to the Turks in 1460. The Venetians were in possession from 1687 to 1715, but neglected it as obsolete and too far from the sea. In 1825 it was partly dismantled by Ibrahim Pasha. At the top there is a polygonal inner ward, with an outer enclosure on the west and north. The inner ward is lined with vaulted buildings two storeys high; on the north side a landing marks the original entrance to the hall, on the south another large room was the chapel, and in the basement at the south-west corner there is a large cistern. Store rooms and living quarters were built against the outer curtain too, though not much is left except fireplaces. Chlemoutsi is the finest Frankish ruin in Greece and still fairly pure in style, though in the outer wall the south-west bastion and the south and west towers are Turkish improvements, designed for artillery, and the parapets too were rebuilt by the Turks.

Glarentza, which used to be a considerable port, lay just north-west of modern Killini. Its port has sanded up and little remains of the Frankish castle and town, destroyed by the Byzantines in 1430 to prevent its use against Chlemoutsi, but at least it is still the titular seat of the duchy of Clarence.

11 · Achaea

Classical Achaea was the northern part of the Peloponnese between Sicyon and Elis, a narrow but rich coastal plain with high mountains behind. The main road, from Corinth through Patras to Pyrgos, keeps to the coast. Car ferries cross the gulf from Rion (near Patras) to Antirion and further east from Aigion (Eyion) to Itea. Patras is the main town and has good hotels.

Very little is known of Achaea before the end of the Bronze Age, when according to tradition Mycenaean refugees settled here. In the Early Iron Age a string of twelve cities grew up, none of much consequence though Helike, submerged in an earthquake of 373 B.C., might illuminate Greek archaeology, if it could be explored. The region first became important after 280 B.C., when the Achaean League was reorganised as a close federation and for more than a century attempted to unify the Peloponnese—on its own terms—till the Romans intervened in 146. Later the name of Achaea was adopted for the whole Roman province of southern Greece, a curious return to the usage of Homer where 'Achaean' is the regular word for 'Greek'.

Patras

In spite of its situation Patras was only a mediocre Achaean city till in 14 B.C. the Romans brought in retired soldiers and developed it as a commercial port. Their vision was justified. Patras managed to acquire St Andrew and with his aid scattered the Slav besiegers in A.D. 805. The Franks came in 1205 and installed a Latin archbishop. From 1408 to 1460 Venice, the Pope and the Byzantines were successively in charge. The Turks followed and except for the Venetian episode of 1687–1715 stayed on till evicted by the French in 1828. The present city was laid out soon after, since at the beginning of the War of Independence Patras had revolted and been burnt in reprisal. It is now the largest place in the Peloponnese and has been given a university.

Patras offers few ancient remains—a rebuilt Roman odeum and an agreeable Museum with contents which interest some specialists. The castle, on the ancient acropolis, is better. Its circuit goes back to the Early Byzantine period, before the Slav invasion, and much of the original work—re-using older material—survives on the north, though the east and south curtains were largely rebuilt by the Franks. The middle tower on the north side of the keep appears Late Byzantine; the tower at the west corner of the outer enclosure may be Venetian of the early fifteenth century; and the gate on the east, the south-east tower, the parapets and various modifications and repairs are Turkish, mostly earlier than 1687. By then the castle was being neglected; it was too vulnerable to modern artillery and the fortress at Rion was strategically more useful.

Rion

The Castle of the Morea, beside the ferry at Rion, is an excellent specimen of an artillery fortress, with its low sloping walls, well placed batteries and wet ditch. It was built by the Turks in 1499 at the same time as the less impressive Castle of Roumeli at Antirion to command the straits between them, here a mile and a quarter across. The Venetians modernised the fortifications between 1687 and 1715, and when in 1828 it surrendered to the liberators—the last Turkish outpost in the Peloponnese—the French made some necessary repairs and improvements.

12 · Delphi and Holy Luke

Delphi is around 1900 feet up on the south side of Mt Parnassus. From Athens there are two good routes, one starting by the National Road and branching off for Thebes, the other starting on the Corinth highway and just past Eleusis turning right—again for Thebes; from Thebes the road to the west goes through Levadhia to Delphi. From the Peloponnese the usual route is by the car ferry from Aigion (Eyion), 25 miles east of Patras, to Itea and up to Delphi by road. Another and more frequent car ferry crosses from Rion (5 miles from Patras) to Antirion and from there a mostly fair road leads east through Navpaktos, Lidhoriki and Amphissa; Navpaktos or Naupactus, which the Franks called Lepanto, has admirable fortifications, in the main Venetian (*Plate* 13). From the north there is a fair road from Lamia

Plate 13. Air view of Naupactus from the south-west.

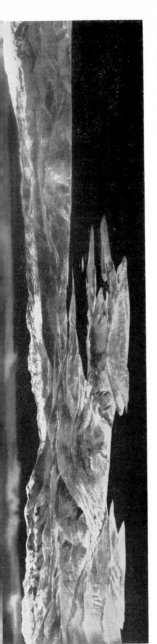
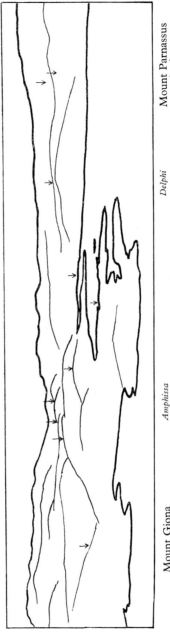

Mount Giona			Delphi	Mount Parnassus
	Amphissa			Arachova
	Ay. Efthimia		Itea	Dhesfina
	Pendeoria	Kolopetinitsa		Mount Cirphis
Vidavi		Galaxidhi		

Plate. 14. Air view (infra-red) of the Gulf of Itea from the south-south-west. The distance across the coast is about 15 miles. The places marked in italics on the key are on or near the sites of independent 'cities' of the Classical period.

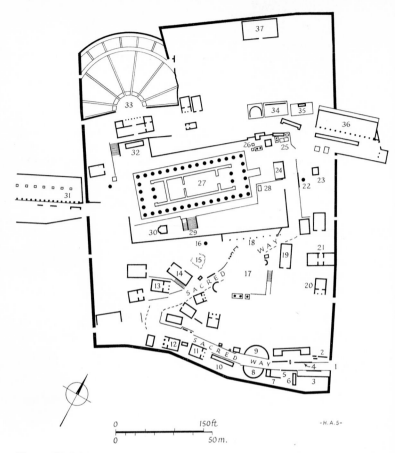

Fig. 29. **Delphi, Sanctuary of Apollo**.

1, main entrance to sanctuary. 2, Bull (Corcyra). 3, Admirals (Sparta). 4, monument (Arcadians). 5, Marathon monument (Athens). 6, Horse (Argos). 7, Seven
against Thebes (Argos). 8, Epigoni (Argos). 9, Kings of Argos (Argos). 10, monument (Tarentum). 11, Sicyonian treasury. 12, Siphnian treasury. 13, Athenian
treasury. 14, Council house (Bouleuterion). 15, Rock of the Sibyl. 16, Column
of the Naxians. 17, Halos ('threshing floor'). 18, Stoa of the Athenians. 19, Corinthian treasury. 20, Cyrenaean treasury. 21, Prytaneum (?). 22, Serpent
column. 23, Chariot of the Rhodians. 24, Altar of the Chians. 25, Tripods of the
Dinomenids. 26, Pillar of Prusias. 27, Temple of Apollo. 28, Pillar of Aemilius
Paulus. 29, spring. 30, early treasury (?). 31, Hellenistic stoa. 32, dedication of
Craterus. 33, Theatre. 34, monument of Daochus. 35, Precinct of Neoptolemos.
36, Stoa of Attalus I. 37, Lesche of the Cnidians.

through Gravia to Amphissa, or as a variation one can cross Parnassus by a tolerable track from Gravia to Arachova (the next village east of Delphi). Delphi has several good hotels.

Amphissa   (*Plates* 14 and *frontispiece*)

The region from Antirion to Amphissa was the Ozolian Locris of the ancients and those who take the western route to Delphi can judge of its importance. Phocis, stretching eastwards to the hills before Levadhia, had good land to the north of Parnassus, but the principal place in the southern parts has usually been Amphissa, though since its name changed to Salona the site may have been deserted at some time during the Slav troubles. The castle and a church at its southern foot are worth seeing. The church, Ayios Soter, with good brick ornament is comparable to that of Chonika and presumably also of the early twelfth century. The castle was built by the Franks about 1205 but passed to the Catalans in 1311 and to the family of Aragon in 1335. The Turks were called in by the local bishop in 1394 and probably kept a small garrison there till the nineteenth century. The lower enclosure at least in part follows the line of the ancient acropolis wall, of which there are considerable remains at the south; in the upper enclosure the round tower at the west end appears earlier than the wall and, if so, should be Byzantine; and the stretch of the lower wall nearest to it may be early Turkish, since it seems designed to take light artillery but in the older fashion is high.

Delphi   (*Figs.* 29 and 30, *Plate* 15)

In its heyday Delphi claimed to be the centre of the world, showing as proof (like other cities so situated) the earth's petrified navel, a domical boulder that stood inside the temple of Apollo. How such a claim could be made can only be guessed. The position of Delphi was remote and inconvenient, its natural wealth was negligible, the settlement which began in the Late Bronze Age remained insignificant, the scenery was not abnormally grand (if indeed the early Greeks had much taste for rugged grandeur) and there were other oracles in central and southern Greece. Presumably some fortunate prophecies gave Delphi a lead and the little village exploited it cleverly. Anyhow by the seventh or later eight century B.C. its oracle of Apollo was pre-eminent in Greece, answering equitably and humanely the problems of private inquirers and also (as far as was prudent) religious and political questions put by the great states, and it became regular to ask the god's blessing on any expedition to found a new city overseas. So at the beginning of the sixth century the Delphians were able to procure their independence under a guarantee from the Amphictyonic Council, appointed by most of the Greek powers that mattered. Even after 479 B.C., when the oracle had unluckily backed the Persians and scepticism was growing, the sanctuary continued to flourish and, though the Phocians melted down many of its treasures in the mid fourth century and the Romans looted works of art in the first centuries B.C. and A.D., there were always new benefactors for a sanctuary so hallowed by tradition. At last in the third century A.D. decline set in, as elsewhere, and the end came in the fourth or fifth century, when Christianity was established as a compulsory religion and Delphi had to live on its own resources. When travellers began to visit Greece in modern times, they found a poor village called Kastri on the site of the sanctuary of Apollo, and the first job of the French excavators in 1892 was to move its inhabitants to their present location. Though at first obstructive, the modern Delphians have become reconciled to the prosperity brought by their forgotten antiquities.

The Sanctuary of Apollo, the principal sanctuary of Delphi, occupies much the same position as the early (and later) villages, part of a steep hollow between high cliffs, liable to landslides as well as earthquakes but with convenient springs. The main entrance is round the south-east corner of the enclosing wall, about 300 yards past the Museum on the main road from the village. Another road above the village climbs to near the Stadium; but though it is easier to walk down the site, on a first visit much of the effect is lost by the wrong approach to the temple. In its final extent, fixed in the later sixth century B.C., the sanctuary was about 200 yards long and 150 wide and the slope was necessarily terraced. In the middle stood a big temple of Apollo and the remaining space was crammed with lesser holy places, treasuries and dedications (mostly statues set singly or in rows on bases and pedestals of every type). Even after Nero's visit there were three thousand such statues to be seen and the general impression must have been like that given by an old-fashioned musuem or an opulent Italian cemetery, though the alignment was less regular and the choice of site governed by more Hellenic principles.

From the main entrance the Sacred Way leads obliquely up; in Greek times it had level stretches and steps (of which traces can be

Plate 15. Delphi before excavation, view from the west (Edward Lear, 1849).

seen on the lower courses of the Altar of the Chians) but under the Romans these were replaced by the present graded slope, though some of the paving was laid by the recent villagers. Much of the first stretch is bordered by bases for statues, now vanished. Just inside the gate on the left was the Spartan monument for their victory over the Athenians in 405–4, erected next to an earlier Athenian memorial of their defeat of the Persians at Marathon; and across the way the Arcadians afterwards found a place for their monument to advertise the humiliation of Sparta in 369. Further on there is a cluster of 'treasuries', built by states in Greece and overseas as repositories for valuable offerings and equipment for embassies. Since treasuries were small and were bound to be compared with one another, they tended to be especially fine or showy in execution and they provide the first buildings in Greece entirely of marble. The Athenian Treasury, dated by its sculpture about 500 B.C. and rebuilt in 1903–6, gives a fair idea of their scale and quality. The Siphnian Treasury, partly reconstructed in the Museum, is a more fancy product in an Ionic style, dedicated about 525 in gratitude for a rich strike of silver in the independent island of Siphnos; the lower part of this treasury still stands below the first corner of the Sacred Way. The Treasury of Sicyon, just before it and again of around 500 B.C., is notable for the remains of two older Doric structures re-used in its foundations; one was a round building of about 580 B.C., the other —perhaps twenty years later—a sort of baldachino (like a temple with colonnade but no cella) to which belong the engaging sculptures in the Museum that are known as the metopes of the Sicyonian Treasury.

In the rocky terrain above the Athenian Treasury there was a little shrine of Ge (or Earth), who legend says preceded Apollo as patron and prophet of Delphi, but in spite of the labours of students of Greek religion we know little if anything more than that. Further on, a prominent rock is perhaps that from which the pious believed that at some unhistorical time the Sibyl foretold the future. Behind it was the Column of the Naxians of about 570 B.C.; some of its drums lie near the spot and the sphinx which surmounted it is in the museum. Next and against the terrace wall of the temple columns of the Athenian Stoa have been re-erected; it contained spoils of naval victories over the Persians and is our best specimen of Ionic architecture of the 470's. On the face of the terrace wall and many other suitable surfaces round the site close inspection shows a network of inscriptions in neat, small lettering—mostly notices of very minor importance. The open space in front of the stoa was the so-called Threshing Floor ('Halos'), where on special occasions ritual dramas were performed. Round the corner and nearly opposite the Altar of the Chians, built in the 470's and now restored, a square base supported the Serpent Column; this was composed of three intertwining bronze snakes with a tripod on their heads and, engraved on their bodies, the names of those Greek states which defeated the Persians at Plataea in 479 B.C. Eight centuries later the column was removed to Constantinople and set up in the Hippodrome, and—improbably—pieces of it have survived. Behind this base stood the chariot of the Rhodians, dedicated probably about 300 B.C.; it has been suggested that the horses of St Mark's, which the Venetians picked up in Constantinople, belonged to this chariot, but all that can be said safely is that they are of the right size and date and very probably came from an important Greek sanctuary. For most of the other statues of Delphi we have at best only the marks of their attachment to the base, which may give some notion of size and pose. One of the most curious is a base just above the Serpent Column, which has sockets for a reaper's feet, his sickle and stalks of corn, and presumably was a thank offering for an exceptional harvest.

We know of three Temples of Apollo. From the character of its remains the first should have been built in the early sixth century, perhaps but not necessarily on the alignment of the later altar, and it was burnt down about 548. During the next generation the terrace was enlarged, covering several earlier structures, and a bigger temple put up; some of its sculpture is in the Museum. When in 373 this temple was demolished by an earthquake and landslide, the present retaining wall ('Ischegaon') was built at the north, making the terrace narrower, and the third temple put up—again with contributions from other Greek states—on much the same site and plan. During the last war the French re-erected some of its columns, giving the ruins that necessary vertical accent which the restored Athenian Treasury is too squat and solid to provide. Part of the building accounts have survived and analyse the cost of stone for the cornice, which was quarried near Corinth; charges at Corinth were 61 drachmas, shipping from Lechaeum to Cirrha 224 drachmas, and haulage from Cirrha up to Delphi 420 drachmas. Roads of course were very bad and haulage was amateurish.

The temple contained the oracle, about which ancient accounts do not tally with the findings of archaeologists nor yet geologists. Admittedly the internal arrangements of the temple are not clear, since it was treated badly in Christian times, perhaps less from religious zeal than because of the general scarcity of useful metal: as can be seen, it was worth levering up large blocks of the foundations to hack out the metal clamps that tied courses together. Geologically, though, it seems impossible that mephitic vapours could have issued from the rocks of Delphi. What is undisputed is that after payment of a fee and sacrifice the client entered the temple and put his question through a priest to the Pythia (or prophetess), who somehow passed into a frenzy, and that her reply, unintelligible to the client, was interpreted by a priest.

In the corner north-east of the temple there were several pillars and paired columns supporting statues, a fashionable dedication of the third and second centuries B.C. That of the Bithynian king Prusias, of about 180 B.C., has been restored, though without its statue. It can be compared with the Monument of Agrippa at Athens. Above and behind the retaining wall the base of the Daochus monument is interesting since it shows how the statues on it were grouped and several of them exist in the Museum. North-west of the temple a stairway goes up to the small Theatre, probably built in the fourth century and restored in the second century B.C. and again in Roman times. Both setting and view are admirable. In the wilderness at the north-east of the sanctuary one can be forgiven for missing the mean and crumbling ruins of houses of the Early Iron Age village.

At the bottom of the Theatre a path, perhaps now blocked by a fence, leads off westwards along the contour, passing the ruins of a big Hellenistic stoa and further on the agreeable modern cemetery to come out at the first corner of the road from the present village to the Stadium. The cemetery is on the site and partly on the foundations of the Synedrion or meeting hall of the Amphictyonic Council, which Hadrian built about 130 A.D. The Stadium can be reached also by a path which winds up from near the top of the Theatre and passes the Classical and Archaic fountain houses of Kerna. It goes back to the mid fifth century B.C., but the stone seating and the triumphal arch at the east were donated by Herodes Atticus in the mid second century A.D. and in their present state make the most charming of his ubiquitous embellishments. The Pythian Games, which were held here, had been reorganised about 590 B.C. as a four-yearly festival, ranking next to the Olympic in prestige, and included musical events. The Hippodrome for horse and chariot races was somewhere at the bottom of the valley, 1700 feet below. On the ridge just west of the Stadium there is a stretch of fortification, put up by the Phocians when they occupied Delphi around 350 B.C. Further down this ridge rock-cut tombs of various dates can be seen; this area, west of the sanctuary of Apollo, was the main burying place of the early village as also of the later town, which was built further down the slope below the sanctuary.

On the other side of the sanctuary of Apollo a mass of ruins have been excavated but not studied. The most curious is the Stoa of Attalus I, of the late third century B.C., which projects into the sanctuary just above the temple. In Roman times it was converted into a cistern. Further on at the bend of the road an ancient fountain house was fed from the Castalian spring, a few yards up the cleft. The basins may be of the sixth century and the pavement of the court, partly restored, of the fourth century B.C.

Across the corner and at the side of the welcome cafe a path branches down to the Gymnasium and on to Marmaria or rather the sanctuary of Athena Pronaia. The Gymnasium was built in the fourth century B.C. and largely rebuilt in the Roman period. It is on two terraces, on the upper of which two race tracks were laid out, one under the cover of a stoa and the other in the open and each nearly 200 yards long— the length of the track in the Stadium. On the lower terrace are ruins

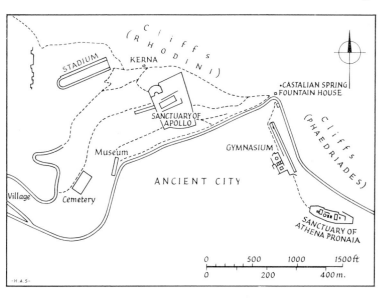

Fig. 30. Delphi, general plan. The upper road on the left winds round nearly to the west end of the stadium.

of a hot bath (added under the Romans), a cold bath with circular swimming pool and basins supplied by spouts in the back wall, and a square colonnaded courtyard ('the palaestra'). In modern times a monastery occupied this site.

The Sanctuary of Athena Pronaia—'Athena before the temple' (of Apollo)—is further along the slope. From west to east the principal ruins are of what is probably a priest's house of the fifth century B.C., the new Temple of Athena of the mid fourth century, the Tholos of about 400, two treasuries (the first perhaps built by the Greek city of Marseilles), the old Temple of Athena, an altar and the entrance gate. The Tholos was a round building of excellent quality and unknown purpose, with a Doric colonnade outside and engaged Corinthian columns inside the central room: part of the outer colonnade has been restored by the French with exemplary taste. Of the treasuries the possibly Massilian, of around 530, was in the 'Aeolic' version of the Ionic style and the other humdrum Doric of the earlier fifth century. The old temple was built near 500, ruined by a landslide (whether about 480 or in 373 or at both times) and abandoned for the new temple; finally in 1905 another landslide destroyed most of the columns which the excavators had just cleared. Some smaller capitals with very flat profile must belong to a still older temple, apparently of the late seventh century, and the quantity of Mycenaean figurines found hereabouts suggests that the place had been holy in the Late Bronze Age.

The Museum is neatly designed in the new style and its selection of the finds is exhibited well. The emphasis rightly is on sculpture. At the top of the stairs there is an unsightly ancient reproduction of the 'omphalos' (Earth's navel), covered with bands of wool. The hall beyond the first gallery contains bronze-work mostly of the seventh century B.C.; a little standing figure, naked except for a belt, is the best example yet known of the male statuary type of the mid seventh century, when Greek sculpture began. In the room beyond there stand the massive statues of Cleobis and Biton, who pulled their mother's ox-cart from Argos to the Argive Heraeum; they are by an Argive sculptor (so the inscription says) and of the very early sixth century. On the wall hang metopes from (but not of) the existing Sicyonian Treasury, neat and mannered reliefs of around 560. The room on the right houses the sphinx from the Column of the Naxians, presumably Naxian work of about 570, the sculpture and partial reconstruction of the Siphnian Treasury, and various oddments. The Siphnian Treasury, put up about 525, was decorated with more exuberance than harmony; the Caryatids that supported the porch are flashy (though the separate head belongs to another and earlier treasury), the pediment with Zeus admonishing Heracles and Apollo as they squabble over the Delphic tripod is clumsily dull, and the frieze—divided between two artists—is in one part elegantly mannered and in the other soberly but admirably up to date with massed figures and rounded modelling. The room on the other side of the hall has the metopes from the Athenian Treasury, about twenty-five years later and an excellent example of the new and revolutionary interest in anatomy; on the Siphnian Treasury all views are strictly frontal or profile, with abrupt 90° swivels between one part of the figure and another, but here torsos twist with the exaggerated emphasis of the pioneering artist. The next room shows the scores of two Delphic hymns, inscribed on blocks from the Athenian Treasury and sadly disillusioning about ancient Greek music, and fragments of one of the pediments of the second Temple of Apollo, mediocre work of the period between the Siphnian and Athenian Treasuries. What is left of the other pediment is in the room on

the right, and the next pair of rooms contain grave reliefs and fragments
of the ceiling and metopes of the Tholos. The wide room beyond has
the sculpture of the Acanthus Column and much of the dedication of
Daochus, but for chronological sequence it is better to pass through
to the end room with the bronze Charioteer. This famous statue was
dedicated about 470 B.C. to commemorate a victory of a Sicilian tyrant
in a chariot race and was buried in some ancient landslide. Compared
even with the Olympia pediments it is a dullish piece, with stupid
face and monotonous folds to the skirt, but these are characteristics of
the very early Classical style which was deliberately severe, and of
course some distraction was offered by the chariot and horses, of which
only a few scraps survive. To go back to the last room, the Acanthus
Column, crowned with three dancers, seems to be dated to the 330's,
a softly charming work though the modelling of the faces is for its
period surprisingly stodgy. Daochus's dedication, also of the 330's, had
a row of nine statues representing (without portraying) members of
his family and six of them survive more or less; they are competent
works, evidently carved by several sculptors but interesting mainly
because they show the range of styles current at the same time. The
gallery along the front of the building contains besides good small
objects a statue of Hadrian's favourite Antinous, set up about A.D.
130 and less sentimental than it seems at first glance. Finally, in the
space at the head of the staircase the sketchily careless frieze from the
monument of Aemilius Paulus, erected in 168 B.C., commemorates the
beginning of Roman suzerainty in Greece. Outside, on the left as one
leaves, a big mosaic floor has been relaid; it comes from a basilical
church which stood within the modern village and is an attractive product of the fifth century A.D. Above this under the trees is a kind of
elephants' graveyard, where the excavators have collected building
blocks from all over the site in the hope (sometimes fulfilled) of fitting
them together.

   To have been to the Corycian cave up on Parnassus gives a certain
prestige. On foot, preferably with a guide, one takes the path above
the Stadium, climbs the scarp and continues, bearing eastwards, on
the plateau till after two hours one passes a chapel on the left and then
a lake (wet or dry according to the season) on the right. Immediately
after the lake at the foot of a steep slope there is or was a battered notice
pointing upwards and a rough path beside it. By this path it is 20 to
25 minutes scramble to the cave. By car one goes to Arachova (notable
for a good and unresinated local wine) and at the beginning of the

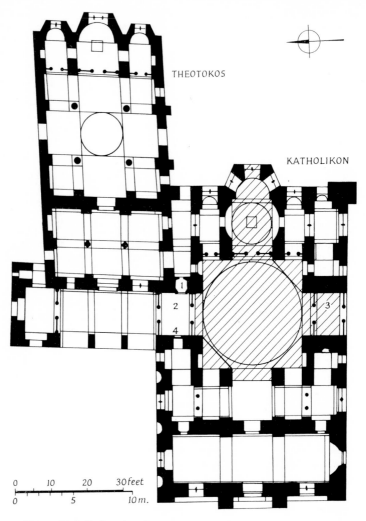

Fig. 31. **Holy Luke,** churches.

1, tomb of Holy Luke. 2–3, mosaics of Christ Pantocrator. 4, mosaic of Holy Luke.

The extent of the crypt is shown by hatching; it is entered outside at the south.

village turns sharply left onto a track which climbs the scarp obliquely. At the top one goes on for a mile or more to a bridge and there forks left—the right fork takes one across Parnassus. In another mile or so at the end of the sunken plain one comes to the notice and the path. The main track is fair, the side track beyond the bridge dangerous after heavy rain. After all this the cave is much like any other big limestone cave, except for its associations.

Holy Luke   (*Fig.* 31)

The monastery of Holy Luke (Osios Loukas) near Stiri is usually approached from the road between Delphi and Levadhia, branching off $15\frac{1}{2}$ miles from Delphi and $14\frac{1}{2}$ from Levadhia at about the spot where legend had Oedipus kill his father. This side road goes to Dhistomo, 2 miles south, and there one turns left and after 8 miles arrives at the monastery. Another though longer route to Delphi crosses Mt Cirphis. One leaves Dhistomo by a moderate track running west to Dhesfina— the destination of the path up the mountainside opposite Delphi—and from there a fair road makes a spectacular and instructive descent to Itea.

Holy Luke was not the evangelist and painter, but a hermit who practised at Stiri, when he was not taking refuge from Bulgarian or Arab raiders, had a chapel built for him, and died about 950. The existing church of the Theotokos may have been begun by Luke himself, the Katholikon (or public church) is of the early eleventh century, the refectory (now rebuilt) cannot be much later, but most of the other monastic structures—except for the lower parts of three towers of the enclosure—are much more recent.

The church of the Theotokos, which was the monastic church, is of cross in square type, curiously askew, with both deep narthex and exonarthex. Its outer walls are decorated busily with regular cloisonné masonry and emphatic brickwork and on the drum of the dome the ornament of the panels has an Islamic flavour. Inside the marble paving survives, but the marble facing of the walls has been robbed; the carved stonework is well preserved; and some early paintings—perhaps of 1100 —still survive.

The Katholikon, fitted onto the corner of the older church to allow access from one to the other, has had some careful restoration, but is the best preserved of the major churches of southern Greece. Like Daphni the wide central dome has eight supports, but unlike Daphni there are galleries (for female pilgrims) over the narthex and the side divisions, so that the play of light and shade is more complex. This second storey is emphasised on the outside by the arrangement of the windows which are more generous than is usual in Greece. Inside the decoration is rich; the walls and floors are embellished with their original slabs of variegated marble and the vaulted ceilings still have their mosaics, except where after damage—as particularly the collapse of the central dome—they have been replaced by paintings. The choice and placing of the subjects are regular and symmetrically balanced; the style differs of course according to the mosaicist, but generally the figures are more squat and severe, their drapery more linear, and the effect less genial than at Daphni. This is not because the mosaicists of Holy Luke were provincial, since in the eleventh century the demand for mosaics in Greece could not have supported a provincial school, and anyhow the style of the Katholikon is sophisticated; one has only to consider the Christ in the north bay with the colouring of the face reversed to counter its shadowed position, and contrast it with the corresponding Christ of the south bay (at 2 and 3 on *Fig.* 31). So the difference between the mosaics of Holy Luke and Daphni must be due to the dates or rather to the personalities of their artists. Below the sanctuary and the central space there is a crypt, dedicated like the hermit's original chapel to St Barbara. It has paintings of the eleventh century in surprisingly good condition.

The monastery is still flourishing, but now that roads and tourism bring so many visitors the monks can no longer offer the old-fashioned hospitality. In compensation a secular cafe has been installed on the terrace, where the modern pilgrim can rest under the plane trees and reflect on the ascetic life while enjoying the same refreshments that he gets at home.

Appendix 1

HISTORICAL SURVEY

The history of Greece till the Middle Bronze Age is reconstructed only from archaeology—an unreliable guide; for the Late Bronze (or Mycenaean) Age we have as well legends written down several hundred years later and hard to interpret; for the Early Iron Age one may also extract something from Homer and make inferences from institutions that survived; but it is only in the Archaic period that historical records begin and till very recent times these are at best patchy. In time a little more should be learnt through archaeology and a fuller examination of documents, but a great deal will always be obscure.

By the Late Neolithic period Greece was settled widely with smallish villages and this pattern continued into the Middle Bronze Age, though there are signs that more powerful units were forming before that period began. If so, they were cut short by the general upsets around 2200 B.C., which are thought to have been caused by invaders who brought the Greek language to Greece. In the sixteenth century, at the beginning of the Late Bronze Age, bigger concentrations of wealth and power appeared, notably at Mycenae. The new civilisation, which is called Mycenaean, spread over the Peloponnese and as far north as Thessaly and seems of a type that was common in the Near East. The country was divided between small states, ruled by autocratic kings and administered by a bureaucracy which kept accounts in the inconvenient syllabic script known as Linear B. Efficient exploitation made the kings wealthy enough to want luxury and art, for which they borrowed mainly from Minoan Crete, but prosperity spread some way down, population appears to have increased, and trade reached as far as Egypt and Sicily. In the thirteenth and twelfth centuries this brilliant civilisation collapsed, for reasons that are not clear, new Greek-speaking peoples (notably the Dorians) came into Greece, and soon after there was widespread emigration to the west coast of Turkey. Though iron was now coming into use the higher arts and techniques vanished and there was no need for writing, foreign trade became rare, and settlements seem to have been smaller and more rustic. Kings were now giving way to

	NEOLITHIC		
3200			
	EH I		
2900			
	EH II	EARLY BRONZE AGE	For mainland Greece the Bronze Age is often called HEL-LADIC, similarly sub-divided
2200			
	EH III		
1900			
	MH	MIDDLE BRONZE AGE	
1575			
	LH I LH II LH IIIA LH IIIB LH IIIC	LATE BRONZE AGE	The late Bronze Age of Greece is also called the MYCE-NAEAN period
1100			
		EARLY IRON AGE	Often called the GEOMETRIC period, which may be divided into a PROTO-GEOMETRIC period (1100–900) and a narrower GEOMETRIC period (900–730)
730			
		ARCHAIC	
480			
		CLASSICAL	CLASSICAL is also used in a wider sense, sometimes equivalent to HELLENIC
323			
		HELLENISTIC	
B.C. 27			
A.D.		ROMAN	
330			

Prehellenic

Hellenic

A.D. 330			
	EARLY BYZANTINE	This division of BY-ZANTINE is not canonical, but convenient for southern Greece. LATE RO-MAN is often used for	Medieval
823	MIDDLE BYZANTINE	the first two or three centuries of what is here called BYZAN-TINE. For Christian manifestations in art and architecture till	
1204	LATE BYZANTINE	the sixth century EARLY CHRISTIAN is sometimes used.	
1453	TURKISH	(This might well be counted as still Medi-eval)	Modern
1829	MODERN GREEK		

NOTE: As reading other books and even labels shows, dates are very uncertain till the Middle Bronze Age, fairly secure for the Late Bronze Age, shaky for the Early Iron Age and much of the Archaic period, and afterwards more or less reliable.

councils of the landed aristocracy, who could afford at least to keep up chariots. The economy was again self-sufficient and there was no pressure from outside.

In the Archaic period which followed Greek society changed fundamentally. The population was growing, anyhow in maritime states, new Greek settlements were founded overseas, especially in Sicily and South Italy, and trade with Syria had revived. This contact with a more advanced civilisation brought the alphabet to Greece, created a taste for luxury and stirred artists to the experiments which produced Greek sculpture and architecture as we know them. Naturally the new prosperity caused political trouble, as fresh classes became able to demand a share of power, and by the fifth century two forms of government were regular—oligarchy, or the rule of the wealthy minority, and democracy, in which more or all of the adult male citizens had an active part. Both oligarchies and democracies had common institutions. A council, usually of at least a hundred, managed or prepared public business; an assembly of all qualified citizens, who might number several thousands, decided major or minor issues; and the executive was split up among annually elected officers. The constitutional struggle was and continued to be bitter, and at one time or another during the seventh and sixth centuries most growing states succumbed to 'tyranny', that is a dictatorship seized by force and, since it was dependent on good will or at least lack of effective opposition, biased towards the smaller men whose interests were democratic. One state, Sparta, was different. There a small ruling group kept its position through a lifelong military discipline and by the later sixth century controlled most of the Peloponnese either through annexation or imposed alliances.

The Classical period begins after the Persian War. In the 540's the Persian Empire had reached the Aegean and subdued the Asiatic Greek cities. When they revolted in 500, Athens (which had just become a democracy) was so impudent as to send them help and in 490 the Persians retaliated. Surprisingly the Athenians defeated the punitive force at Marathon. Ten years later the Persians invaded Greece in earnest and Sparta naturally took the lead in resisting them, though by now Athens ranked second as the biggest naval power. Two lucky victories, one at sea off Salamis and the other on land at Plataea, forced the Persians to withdraw and, since Sparta was reluctant, Athens took the opportunity to liberate the Asiatic Greeks and build up a naval empire. So Sparta and Athens became the two great powers, supported respectively by oligarchs and democrats in other states, and in the Peloponnesian

War (431–404) they fought it out. As it happened, Sparta won—with Persian help—but its use of supremacy soon provoked opposition and in 371 the Spartan empire was destroyed by Thebes. The subsequent bids for domination—for aggression was a characteristic of the Greek city-state—were ended in 338, when Philip II of the despised and semi-barbarous kingdom of Macedonia made himself master of Greece. His son, Alexander the Great, was equally effective.

With Alexander the Hellenistic period began. After making sure of Greece he turned east and conquered the Persian Empire, but died young in 323 without a competent heir. His generals, though, were competent and after some very professional warfare divided his possessions into large kingdoms for themselves, of which Egypt, Syria, Pergamum and Macedonia were or became the most important. Greece itself was now a backwater, useful as a source of skilled personnel, civil as well as military, and venerable for its culture, while the various states usually had enough independence to continue fighting each other. In the second century Rome made its first direct intervention, which led on to more effective but piecemeal control, and in 27 B.C. Greece was organised definitely as part of the Roman Empire. By then many of the Classical cities had been destroyed and their place was taken by big estates, but peace and its cultural and educational prestige brought some increase in prosperity, especially (as the ruins show) in the second century A.D.

From the mid third century onwards barbarian raiders kept breaking into Greece and the shrunken cities began to fortify themselves again. The removal of the capital in 330 from Rome to Byzantium (renamed Constantinople) gave more protection, but as the Empire became more dogmatically Christian, Greece became provincial even in culture and in the seventh century with Slav invasion on land and Arab piracy by sea the Byzantine authorities lost control of most of its southern part except for a few coastal strongholds. It was two or three hundred years before the Slavs (and the Greeks of the Mani) began to be converted and absorbed and Greece itself revived, but soon the central power weakened again and by the twelfth century local magnates (or 'archons') were becoming virtually independent, like Leon Sgouros of Nauplia whose private army captured Argos and Corinth. So when in 1204 the Fourth Crusade seized Constantinople and Frankish adventurers attacked Greece, most of its inhabitants were ready to change masters. In southern Greece two Frankish states were formed, the Principality of the Morea (or Peloponnese) and the Duchy of Athens and Thebes, both soon autonomous since their feudal superiors were reconquered by the Byzantines. To hold their possessions the Franks built modern castles, sometimes remodelling old citadels, and these are now among the best preserved and most neglected ruins in Greece. In its heyday the Frankish court of the Morea was one of the most chivalrous in Christendom—of the Roman persuasion—but this did not endear it to its Orthodox subjects. The first disaster came in 1259 when the ruling prince of the Morea was captured in an invasion of Byzantine territory and as ransom had to cede his strongholds in the south-east Peloponnese. From these bases, and particularly Mistra, the Byzantines slowly recovered the rest. The Duchy of Athens had its troubles too, but remained independent.

The Turks arrived near the end of the fourteenth century, but waited till 1460 before they finally annexed southern Greece, except for some Venetian bases (most acquired as spoils of the Fourth Crusade) which held out as late as 1540 on the mainland and longer in the islands. After the last spasms of Byzantine government the Turks were often welcome and at first their rule was relatively mild, but gradually corruption and incompetence with occasional bouts of savagery made them as unpopular as any of their predecessors and much of the fertile lowland was deserted by the peasants and ceased to provide revenue. Albanians had been invited into Greece from the later fourteenth century on, and more were brought in by the Turks till they occupied most of Boeotia, Attica and the Argolid; but though Albanian is still spoken in some outlying villages, these foreigners (like the Slavs) have been assimilated. They had no national tradition of their own and are now as conscious as any other Greeks of their Hellenic heritage.

For three centuries after the Turkish conquest there was no serious thought of a free Greece. In the mountains the local chiefs were left more or less to themselves, and in the towns and plains many of the higher clergy and laymen made profitable arrangements with their rulers. So there was little support for the Venetians when as partners in a grand alliance they took the Peloponnese and Attica between 1685 and 1715 but were too weak to keep them. Soon afterwards Russia began to champion Orthodox Christians elsewhere as part of its imperialist strategy and in 1770 promoted a revolution in the Peloponnese; but Russian help was negligible and most of the Peloponnesians stayed quiet, so that the principal result was the burning of Mistra. A few years afterwards the French Revolution had its invigorating effect and the idea of Greek independence began to be propagated, especially by the prosperous colonies of Greeks outside the Turkish Empire. Finally in 1821 revolution broke out generally in the Peloponnese and sporadically further north, and many of the islanders joined enthusiastically. By Western standards the War of Independence was shockingly conducted. On land the Greeks were badly armed, undisciplined and led by mountain chiefs too jealous of each other to combine, and though the Turks had far bigger resources of men and materials their organisation and methods were still less efficient; even the modernised army of Ibrahim Pasha, who came from Egypt in 1825 to help the Sultan or himself, could not put down the Greek guerillas. By sea the Greek islanders showed brilliance, demoralising the better armed Turkish fleet and hampering the Egyptian. At last in 1827 Britain, France and Russia agreed that an autonomous Greece would not upset the balance of Europe and after the naval battle of Navarino and a French military campaign a Greek state was formally recognised in 1829.

The new Greek state was small, comprising the Peloponnese, continental Greece up to the gulfs of Arta and Volo, Euboea and the nearer islands of the Aegean. Since the various factions could not unite—and indeed the provisional president was murdered by rival leaders at Nauplia—it seemed wiser to bring in a foreign king. The choice fell on Otho, a Bavarian prince, passionately philhellenic but very young and inexperienced. The first task was to establish order throughout the country and, since many of the Greek notables felt that they had fought to free themselves not only from the Turks but from any higher authority, Otho relied on Bavarian troops and advisers for his first ten years. In 1862 a second revolt forced him to retire to his homeland, where he still displayed his love of Greece by wearing the fustanella. The new king, a Danish prince, was also young but cannier and left government to the new generation of Greeks. On the whole there was progress towards order and stability, though hampered by two special difficulties —political corruption, which is said to survive still, and the patriotic demand that northern Greece, the larger islands and even Constantinople should be liberated. By themselves the Greeks could not beat the Turks, though the Great Powers conceded Thessaly and a special status for Crete; but the shifting alliances of the two Balkan Wars of 1912–13 gave them parts of Epirus and Macedonia, the eastern Aegean islands except the Dodecanese (which Italy had just seized) and Crete. The First World War brought permission to annex most of the rump of Turkey in Europe and a large area round Smyrna, but the Turks revived and in 1922 drove the Greek armies out, conscientiously massacring those civilians who could not escape. So Greece was left with a piece of Thrace and one and a half million refugees, in part the descendants of the colonists of the Early Iron Age. This disaster had its benefits; exchange of populations made the land frontiers at last rational and the refugees were technically more skilled than the European Greeks and improved the economy. In the Second World War Greece defeated an Italian invasion, but could not defeat the Germans, and from 1941 to 1944 was an occupied country, though even German efficiency did not control the mountains. Afterwards the Dodecanese was annexed and till 1949 there was a civil war, basically a struggle for or against Communism, and especially bitter in the north. Since then the prosperity of Greece has advanced at an extraordinary speed, at first through American aid applied productively, then by budgeted programmes, the great growth of tourism and the demand of German industry for foreign labour. Though there is still much poverty, Greece is changing fast and the old-fashioned peasant is at last disappearing, lamented of course by irresponsible enthusiasts who do not have to endure his miserable existence and still less his wife's.

Appendix 2

NOTES ON TRAVEL

These notes obviously contain personal opinions and omit most of the information that can be got from competent Travel Agents. A useful compendium is the *Key Travel Guide*, published monthly in Athens and including particulars (with prices) of the better hotels and camping sites, time-tables and fares of train, air, ship and car-ferry services in Greece, some bus time-tables, and lists and costs of coach tours. The Greek National Tourist Office also issue a list of hotels, but though more complete this seems less reliable on prices.

Time of Visit

October is the best season for a visit to southern Greece, except for the mountains; the weather is warm and settled, showers have brought out grass and flowers again, and tourists are relatively few. November is nearly as good. The spring, which is usually recommended, may be stormy and cannot be predicted, since it can come as early as March or as late as May.

Routes to Greece

By road the cheapest and easiest route is through Belgrade. The drive can be shortened from late May till late September by the car sleeper services from Ostend or the Hook to Villach in southern Austria.

Travel in Greece

The railway system is not extensive (see *Fig.* 1). Internal air lines are useful for some routes, but hardly serve the Peloponnese. Buses run to almost every town and village and seats can be booked for long journeys, but the hours of return are not always convenient: the KTEL time-tables are complete and accurate. Coach tours round the main archaeological sites are run by several agencies in Athens; the charges include board and lodging and a polyglot guide. Reliable car-hire firms exist in Athens and arrangements can be made from abroad through a good travel agent. If one brings one's own car, Greek garages are competent.

Roads are being improved faster than they deteriorate; the conditions mentioned in this book were checked in summer 1966. Road maps also should not be trusted too much; those we have seen omit some or many minor roads and tracks and may include others that do not exist, like that from Phyle towards Thebes, but one can always ask.

If animals are hired, donkeys and mules are usually better than horses on rough paths. On the normal saddle one should sit sideways.

Hotels

All towns have hotels of one sort or another. They are graded in five main categories, Luxury (or AA) and A to D, of which A and B regularly provide private baths or showers and often hot water. Rooms can be booked by phone.

Food and Drink

Greek cuisine is not distinguished. Tourist restaurants and the restaurants attached to many hotels of the A and B categories outside Athens tend to serve mediocre food of international type. For good Greek cooking it is safest to try large old-fashioned restaurants. Tavernas vary and are liable to be spoilt quickly by success; the pleasantest are usually by the sea, though fish is unexpectedly dear. The waiter's tip is included in the bill, but the boy assisting him should be given a small sum.

Most local wines are resinated, but the average foreigner learns to tolerate the taste after about a gallon and anyhow there is a variety of moderate unresinated table wines. Water is generally safe and often good; the diarrhoea that many visitors attribute to it comes usually from too much fruit or oil.

Shopping

Shopping hours are 8.30 a.m.—1.30 p.m. and 4.30—7.30 p.m. from November to April, 5—8 p.m. from May to October. Usually half-day closing is on Saturday, except for groceries which take Wednesday. Most international goods are on sale in large towns, though prices are higher for imports.

Archaeological Sites etc.

Most major and some minor sites are fenced in; generally opening hours are from October to April 9 a.m. till sunset, and from May till September 7.30 a.m. till sunset. Museums vary more in their times; from October to April 9 a.m.—4 p.m. is common in Athens and 9 a.m.—1 p.m. and 2.30—5 p.m. elsewhere; from May to September 9 a.m.—5 p.m. or 8 a.m.—1 p.m. and 3—6 p.m. are usual in Athens and 9 a.m.—1 p.m. and 3—6 p.m. or 2—5 p.m. elsewhere; the normal closing day is Monday, though the Acropolis Museum and the Benaki Museum in Athens have Tuesday mornings, and there are shorter hours on Sundays and holidays. Generally photography is permitted, though in museums only without a tripod and at the cost of an extra ticket. A regulation, sometimes enforced very strictly, forbids the removal of any part of the Greek cultural heritage, which can include the smallest fragment of pottery. In churches reasonably informal behaviour is accepted, but women should wear something more conventional than shorts and cover their shoulders and they are forbidden to enter the sanctuary. If a guide is hired, the women are often better informed than the men, though less facetious.

Language

English is understood widely, but when travelling it is useful to have a phrase book and very useful to be able to read the Greek alphabet. On main roads direction signs usually give names both in Greek and transliterated into the Western alphabet (though not rendered into any Westernised form), but on minor roads signs are often written only in Greek. A key to transliteration and pronunciation is offered in *Table* 2; it should be used elastically, since Greek usage is not consistent nor has ours been in this book. For practice in the technique of transliteration, one cannot do better than look at Greek advertisements for foreign films and puzzle out the names of the stars.

TABLE 2: **The Greek Alphabet**

NAME (*English*)	FORM Capital	Small	TRANSLITERATION	PRONUNCIATION (*if not obvious from transliteration*)
Alpha	A	α	A	between *a* in *can't* and *cat*, or sometimes as *u* in *cut*.
	AI	αι	AI or E	near *e* in *get*
	AΥ	αυ	{ AV before voiced sounds / AF before F,K,P,S,T,TH,χ	
Beta	B	β	V	
Gamma	Γ	γ	{ GH before α (but not αι), ο, ου, ω / Y before other vowels	a voiced form of the *ch* of *loch* (between it and the uvular fricative *r* used in Northumberland)
	ΓΓ	γγ	NG	as *ng* in *finger*
	ΓΚ	γκ	{ G at beginning of word / NG elsewhere	
	ΓΞ	γξ	NX	
	Γχ	γχ	NG+χ	
Delta	Δ	δ	DH	as *th* in *then*
Epsilon	E	ε	E	near *e* in *get*
	EI	ει	I	as *i* in *machine*
	EΥ	ευ	{ EV before voiced sounds / EF before F,K,P,S,T,TH,χ	
Zeta	Z	ζ	Z	
Eta	H	η	I	as *i* in *machine*
Theta	Θ	θ	TH	as *th* in *thin*
Iota	I	ι	I	as *i* in *machine*
Kappa	K	κ	K	
Lambda	Λ	λ	L	
Mu	M	μ	M	
	MΠ	μπ	{ B at the beginning of word / MB elsewhere	
Nu	N	ν	N	
	NT	ντ	{ D at beginning of word / ND elsewhere	
Xi	Ξ	ξ	X	
Omicron	O	ο	O	as *o* in *or*
	OI	οι	I	as *i* in *machine*
	OΥ	ου	OU	as *u* in *rule*
Pi	Π	π	P	

Rho	P	ρ	R	lightly trilled
Sigma	Σ	σ	S	as *ss* in *ass;* except that before G,M,N and V it is as *s* in *easy*
		ς (at end of word)		
Tau	T	τ	T	
Upsilon	Υ	υ	I	as *i* in *machine*
	ΥΙ	υι	I	as *i* in *machine*
Phi	Φ	φ	F or PH	
Chi	X	χ	CH or H	before α (but not αι), ο, ου, ω as *ch* in *loch;* before other vowels as *ch* in German *ich*
Psi	Ψ	ψ	PS	
Omega	Ω	ω	O	as *o* in *or*

Dipthongs are split as far as possible into their component vowels: so αϊ (=*i* in *fine*) and εϊ (=*a* in *Faber*, which would though be pronounced *Fameber*). For foreign sounds not current in Greek the nearest approximation is made: so one renders English *ch* by τζ, *h* by χ, *j* by τζ, *sh* by σ (or ς), *w* by ου. The accents ´ ` ˆ show the stress, but the difference between them are only learned survivals. The breathings ' ' that accompany initial vowels are also survivals and not pronounced. In punctuation ; is a question mark.

As can be seen, the pronunciation of Greek has changed since this alphabet came into use more than 2500 years ago.

Appendix 3

CONVERSION OF BRITISH AND CONTINENTAL MEASURES

1 inch = about $2\frac{1}{2}$ cm. 1 foot = about 30 cm.

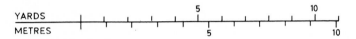

1 metre = about $39\frac{1}{3}$ inches.

8 kilometres = about 5 miles.

1 lb. = about 0.45 kilo. 1 kilo = about $2\frac{1}{5}$ lb.

British

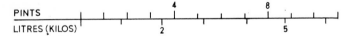

1 litre = about $1\frac{3}{4}$ pints. $\frac{6}{10}$ litre = about 1 pint. The litre is called a kilo in Greece. Greek garages sell petrol in British gallons ('ghalonia').

American

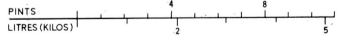

1 litre = about $2\frac{1}{9}$ pints. The litre is called a kilo in Greece. Greek garages sell gas in British gallons (=about $1\frac{1}{5}$ American).

WOMEN'S SHOES			WOMEN'S STOCKINGS		WOMEN'S DRESSES		
B	C	A	AB	C	B	C	A
4	37	$5\frac{1}{2}$	8	0	36	42	8–9
5	38	$6\frac{1}{2}$	$8\frac{1}{2}$	1	38	44	10–11
6	39	$7\frac{1}{2}$	9	2	40	46	12–13
7	41	$8\frac{1}{2}$	$9\frac{1}{2}$	3	42	48	14–15
8	42	$9\frac{1}{2}$	10	4	44	50	16–17
9	43	$10\frac{1}{2}$	$10\frac{1}{2}$	5	46	52	18–19

MEN'S SHOES			MEN'S SOCKS		MEN'S SHIRTS	
B	C	A	AB	C	AB	C
6	39	$6\frac{1}{2}$	$9\frac{1}{2}$	39	$14\frac{1}{2}$	37
7	41	$7\frac{1}{2}$	10	40	15	38
8	42	$8\frac{1}{2}$	$10\frac{1}{2}$	41	$15\frac{1}{2}$	39
9	43	$9\frac{1}{2}$	11	42	16	41
10	44	$10\frac{1}{2}$	$11\frac{1}{2}$	43	$16\frac{1}{2}$	42
11	45	$11\frac{1}{2}$	12	44	17	43

A = American sizes; B = British sizes; C = Continental sizes.

These tables cannot always be relied on, and it is often useful to have one's own tape measure.

Bibliography

History

E. VERMEULE, *Greece in the Bronze Age* (Univ. of Chicago, Chicago, 1964). The most coherent general account, though of course provisional.

LORD WM TAYLOUR, *The Mycenaeans* (Thames and Hudson, London, 1964; Frederick A. Praeger, New York, 1964). A useful introduction.

R. M. COOK, *The Greeks till Alexander* (Thames and Hudson, London, 1961; Frederick A. Praeger, New York, 1962). A short general survey from the 11th to the 4th century B.C.

A. R. BURN, *The Pelican History of Greece* (Penguin Books, Harmondsworth, England and Baltimore, Md., 1966). A convenient account of the history of Greece from Neolithic to Roman times, but concentrating on the Archaic and Classical periods.

A. BON, *Le Péloponnèse byzantin* (Presses Universitaires, Paris, 1951). A good general account.

D. M. NICOL, *Meteora* (Chapman and Hall, London, 1963). A well written study of Orthodox monasticism.

W. MILLER, *The Latins in the Levant* (Barnes and Noble, New York, 1964: reprint of edition of 1908). A detailed study.

J. MAVROGORDATO, *Modern Greece* (Macmillan, London, 1931). Well written, but partial and stops at 1931.

W. A. HEURTLEY, H. C. DARBY, C. W. CRAWLEY and C. M. WOODHOUSE, *A Short History of Greece* (Cambridge Univ. Press, Cambridge, 1965). The modern sections, which go down to 1964, are the more useful.

Art

G. M. A. RICHTER, *A Handbook of Greek Art* (Phaidon Press, London, 1959). Systematic and useful.

J. BOARDMAN, *Greek Art* (Thames and Hudson, London, 1964; Frederick A. Praeger, New York, 1964). A handy introduction.

W. B. DINSMOOR, *The Architecture of Ancient Greece* (Batsford, London, 1950). A detailed account.

A. W. LAWRENCE, *Greek Architecture* (Penguin Books, Harmondsworth, England and Baltimore, Md., 1957). Uneven, but better illustrated and gives more space to the Bronze Age.

R. LULLIES and M. HIRMER *Greek Sculpture* (Thames and Hudson, London, 1960). A sound and well illustrated introduction.

A. W. LAWRENCE, *Classical Sculpture* (Jonathan Cape, London, 1929). An intelligent account, though weak on Archaic.

R. CARPENTER, *Greek Sculpture* (Univ. of Chicago, Chicago, 1960). A provocative and valuable analysis.

A. LANE, *Greek Pottery* (Faber and Faber, London, 1963). A good introduction.

R. M. COOK, *Greek Painted Pottery* (Methuen, London, 1966). A more detailed account.

R. A. HIGGINS, *Greek and Roman Jewellery* (Methuen, London, 1961). A useful survey, which includes the Bronze Age.

R. KRAUTHEIMER, *Early Christian and Byzantine Architecture* (Penguin Books, Harmondsworth, England and Baltimore, Md., 1965). A useful survey, though Greece has only a small part and much is provisional.

O. DEMUS, *Byzantine Mosaic Decoration* (Kegan Paul, London, 1948). An intelligent introduction.

M. CHATZIDAKIS and A. GRABAR, *Byzantine and Early Medieval Painting* (Weidenfeld and Nicolson, London, 1965; The Viking Press, New York, 1965). A short provisional survey.

K. ANDREWS, *Castles of the Morea* (American School of Classical Studies, Princeton N.J., 1953). A good and generously illustrated, though not always reliable, account of castles connected with the Venetians.

Travel

O. LANCASTER, *Classical Landscape with Figures* (Murray, London, 1947; Houghton Mifflin, Boston, 1963). Witty and shrewd, though in part dated.

A. B. CHRISTIE, *Motoring and Camping in Greece* (Faber and Faber, London, 1965). Sound and informative, though already needing revision.

L. FINER, *Passport to Greece* (Longmans, London, 1964; Doubleday, New York, 1965). A sensible and lively account of modern Greek life.

Index